Computing Made Simple

Access 2000
STEPHEN
50641827   1999

Access 2000 Business Edition
STEPHEN
5064611X   1999

Access 97 for Windows
STEPHEN
50638001   1997

CompuServe 2000 NEW!
BRINDLEY
50645245   2000

Designing Internet Home Pages
2nd edition
HOBBS
50644761   1999

ECDL/ICDL Version 3.0 NEW!
BCD
50651873   2000

Excel 2000
MORRIS
50641800   2000

Excel 2000 Business Edition
MORRIS
50646098   2000

Excel 97 for Windows
MORRIS
50638028   1997

Excel for Windows 95 (V. 7)
MORRIS
50628162   1996

Explorer 5
MCBRIDE, P K
50646276   1999

Frontpage 2000
MCBRIDE, Nat
50645989   1999

FontPage 97
MCBRIDE, Nat
50639415   1998

iMac and iBook NEW!
BRINDLEY
5064608X   2000

Internet In Colour
2nd edition
MCBRIDE, P K
50645768   1999

Internet for Windows 98
MCBRIDE, P K
0750645636   1999

MS DOS
SINCLAIR
0750620692   1994

Office 2000
MCBRIDE, P K
0750641797   1999

Office 97
MCBRIDE, P K
0750637986   1997

Outlook 2000 NEW!
MCBRIDE, P K
0750644141   2000

Photoshop
WYNNE-POWELL
075064334X   1999

Pocket PC NEW!
PEACOCK
0750649003   2000

Powerpoint 2000
STEPHEN
0750641770   1999

Powerpoint 97 for Windows
STEPHEN
0750637994   1997

Publisher 2000
STEPHEN
0750645970   1999

Publisher 97
STEPHEN
0750639431   1998

Sage Accounts
McBRIDE
0750644133   1999

Searching the Internet
MCBRIDE, P K
0750637943   1998

Windows 98 NEW!
MCBRIDE, P K
0750640391   1998

Windows 95
MCBRIDE, P K
0750623063   1995

Windows CE
PEACOCK
0750643358   1999

Windows ME NEW!
MCBRIDE, P K
0750652373   2000

Windows NT
HOBBS
0750635118   1997

Word 2000
BRINDLEY
0750641819   1999

Word 2000 Business Edition
BRINDLEY
0750646101   2000

Word 97 for Windows
BRINDLEY
075063801X   1997

Word 7 for Windows 95
BRINDLEY
0750628154   1996

Works 2000
MCBRIDE, P K
0750649852   2000

UPCOMING in 2001

Basic Computer Skills
SHERMAN
075064897X

ECDL/ICDL 3.0
Office 2000 Edition
BCD
0750653388

Microsoft Project 2000
MURPHY
0750651903

ALL YOU NEED TO GET STARTED!

MADE SIMPLE
BOOKS

Programming Made Simple

C Programming
SEXTON
0750632445   1997

C++ Programming
SEXTON
0750632437   1997

COBOL
SEXTON
0750638346   1998

Delphi Version 5   NEW!
MORRIS
0750651881   2000

Delphi
MORRIS
0750632461   1997

HTML 4.0
MCBRIDE
0750641789   1999

Java
MCBRIDE, P K
0750632410   1997

Javascript
MCBRIDE, P K
0750637978   1997

Pascal
MCBRIDE, P K
0750632429   1997

Visual Basic
MORRIS
0750632453   1997

Visual C++
MORRIS
0750635703   1998

UPCOMING in 2001

Visual Basic Version 6
MORRIS
075065189X

ALL
YOU NEED
TO GET
STARTED!

MADE SIMPLE
BOOKS

Project 2000
Made Simple

Brendan Murphy

MADE SIMPLE
BOOKS

OXFORD · AUCKLAND · BOSTON · JOHANNESBURG · MELBOURNE · NEW DELHI

Made Simple
An imprint of Butterworth-Heinemann
Linacre House, Jordan Hill, Oxford OX2 8DP
225 Wildwood Avenue, Woburn MA 01801-2041
A division of Reed Educational and Professional Publishing Ltd

R   A member of the Reed Elsevier plc group

First published 2001
© Brendan Murphy 2001

TRADEMARKS/REGISTERED TRADEMARKS
Computer hardware and software brand names mentioned in this book are
protected by their respective trademarks and are acknowledged.

British Library Cataloguing in Publication Data
A catalogue record for this book is available from the British Library

ISBN 0 7506 5190 3

Typeset by Elle and P.K. McBride, Southampton

Icons designed by Sarah Ward © 1994
Printed and bound in Great Britain

Contents

Preface IX

1 Getting started   1

Opening Project 2000 2

Project properties 4

Saving your project 5

The Gantt Chart view 7

Adding tasks 8

Project calendar 9

Task durations 10

Task notes 11

Printing your project 12

Closing Project 2000 13

Summary 14

2 Working with views   15

Project 2000 views 16

Calendar view 17

The Gantt Chart view 18

Changing the fiscal year 20

Network Diagram view 21

Task usage view 22

Resource Usage view 23

Summary 24

3 Getting Help   25

Using Help 26

The Help index 27

ScreenTips 28

Using Office Assistant 29

Project Help on the Web 30

Wizards 31

Summary 32

4	Project building blocks	33

Project objectives.. 34

Creating a task list 35

Recurring tasks 36

Summary tasks 37

Outlining a task list 38

Outline numbering 39

Splitting tasks 40

The critical path 41

Summary 42

5	Managing resources	43

Project resources 44

Creating a resource list 45

Using a resource pool 47

Changing your calendar 49

Multiple-base calendars 50

Project assignments... 51

Resource levelling 54

Summary 56

6	Linking tasks	57

Linking tasks 58

Different task links 59

Lag and lead times 60

Constraints 62

Summary 64

7	Project costs	65
	Resource rates	66
	Wage rate rises	71
	Project baseline	72
	Checking costs	73
	Summary	76

8	Formatting projects	77
	Changing task names	78
	Working with fields	80
	Formatting text	84
	Formatting Gantt Charts	85
	Sorting project tasks	87
	Summary	88

9	Project charts	89
	Producing project charts	90
	The Gantt Chart view	91
	Calendar view	92
	Network diagram	93
	Resource Sheet view	94
	Resource Graph view	95
	Resource Name Form	96
	The Task Usage view	97
	Task Details form	98
	Tracking Gantt view	99
	Resource Usage view	100
	Filtering information	101
	Summary	104

10	Keeping on track	105
	Project baselines	106
	Project information	107
	Saving an interim plan	109
	Monitoring project tasks	110
	Monitoring project costs	113
	Summary	114

11	Multiple projects	115
	Multiple projects	116
	Creating a master project	117
	Viewing a master project	119
	Deleting sub-projects	121
	Summary	124

12	Sharing information	125
	Copy Picture	126
	Linking with Word	128
	Saving projects as HTML	130
	Inserting an image	131
	Summary	132

	Index	133

Preface

Project management is the art of managing the tasks, resources and costs used in a project to ensure that it is completed satisfactorily, on time and within budget.

You probably use project management techniques almost daily even though you often don't realise that you are applying them. Think about an average day's work. You will likely have a list of jobs that need completed (maybe a 'To Do' list in your diary software) and you will have an idea of how long each job will take and what resources you need to complete each job. At the end of each day or week you'll review your list and take steps to redefine jobs and reprioritise work. You're also likely to communicate those completed jobs to colleagues and clients as well as informing them of the jobs that are likely to take a little longer to complete than was originally expected. In essence, this is project management – even though you probably didn't know it! Project management techniques simply formalise the process.

Project management brings many benefits to you in the business environment. It allows you to:

- track the progress of a project;
- manage resources more effectively;
- ensure a standard method of project delivery is adopted making it easier to manage multiple projects;
- pre-empt problems and take corrective action;
- define and redefine the scope of a project;
- communicate effectively with colleagues and clients;
- project a professional image to clients and other stakeholders.

All of the above benefits are now much easier to realise using project management software.

Using project management software

Although software takes all of the drudge out of project management, great project management starts with a well thought-out and logical plan usually written down on paper first.

Don't be fooled into thinking that project management software is only used in large complex projects involving lots of people, money and resources. It can be effectively deployed in all sizes and types of projects. Indeed, in small projects where resources are tight, you might find that it is invaluable in helping you effectively deliver a finished product or service within an agreed budget and timescale.

In the past, project management was often a difficult, time-consuming and specialist task. However, with the proliferation of the PC, and in particular with the availability of excellent project management software such as Microsoft Project 2000, it's never been easier to deploy effective project management in your business.

What is Microsoft Project 2000?

Project 2000 is a powerful application that provides you with a focused method of managing tasks, resources and project costs. It's straightforward to use and makes the whole process of project management easy and fun.

Project 2000 is the latest version of Microsoft's world beating project management software application. It sits alongside other applications such as Excel, Word, Access, PowerPoint, Outlook, Publisher, FrontPage and PhotoDraw as part of the Microsoft Office 2000 suite. Microsoft Project 2000 provides you with all the tools you need to successfully manage all sizes and complexity of projects.

New in Project 2000

❑ You can now include material resources in your project.

❑ A task can now have a deadline date entered. You can then be alerted if the task is going to finish after this date.

❑ A task's duration can now be estimated.

❑ Tasks and resources can be grouped.

❑ Project templates are provided to allow you to clone a project.

❑ Better options for working with others over the Web are now included.

❑ Better Help systems including detailed lessons on the basics are provided.

1 Getting started

Opening Project 2000 2

Project properties 4

Saving your project 5

The Gantt Chart view 7

Adding tasks 8

Project calendar 9

Task durations 10

Task notes 11

Printing your project 12

Closing Project 2000 13

Summary 14

Opening Project 2000

You can start Project 2000 by clicking on the Start button and choosing Microsoft Project from the Programs menu. The main Project 2000 window will be displayed. Alongside this screen the Help system is displayed.

● By default, Microsoft Project presents a new project ready to be developed.

Creating a new project file

Once you've opened Project 2000 the first thing you'll want to do is start building a new project.

Basic steps

1 From the File menu, select New...

2 Choose the Blank Project template.

3 Click OK.

> ### Tip
>
> You can click the New icon on the Standard toolbar to create a new project.

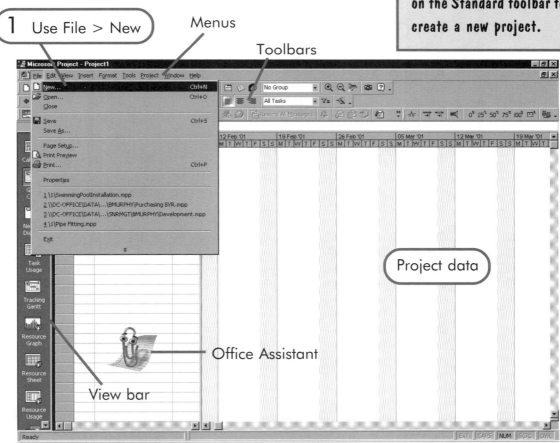

1 Use File > New

Menus

Toolbars

Project data

Office Assistant

View bar

4 From the Project Information dialog box enter details of the dates and calendars used for the project.

5 Decide to track your project from either the start or finish date.

❑ If you choose to track your project from the start date then the finish date box will be unavailable.

❑ If you choose to track your project from the finish date then the start date box will be unavailable.
Select the Standard calendar. This will give your project a standard working week.

6 Click OK.

❑ Instead of choosing the Blank Project template, click on the Project Templates tab and choose one of the pre-defined templates that suits your needs.

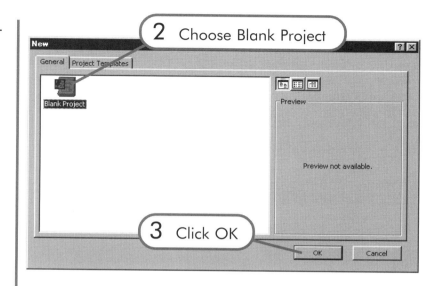

2 Choose Blank Project

3 Click OK

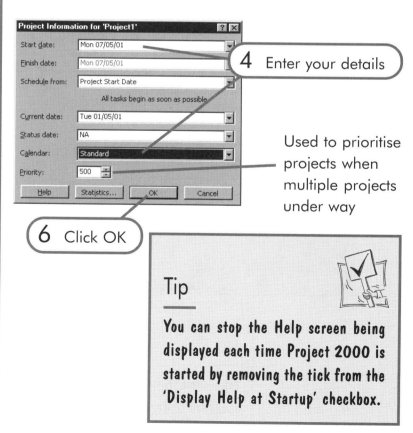

4 Enter your details

6 Click OK

Used to prioritise projects when multiple projects under way

Tip

You can stop the Help screen being displayed each time Project 2000 is started by removing the tick from the 'Display Help at Startup' checkbox.

Project properties

Set the basic details of your project. Concentrate on completing entries listed in the Summary tab.

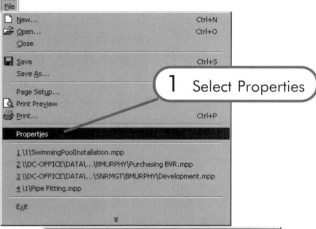

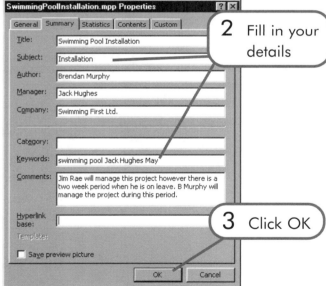

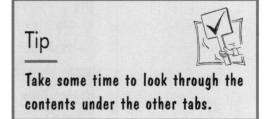

Take some time to look through the contents under the other tabs.

1 From the File menu, select Properties and open the Summary tab.

2 Enter these details:

   a suitable title;

   its subject;

   the author's name;

   the name of the manager responsible;

   your company name;

   some keywords that can be used when searching for this project;

   any relevant comments.

3 Click OK.

Tip

You can search for a project, using keywords, from the Tools menu in the File Open dialog box.

Saving your project

Once you've created a new project and set up some basic project information the next thing to do is to save it in an appropriate folder.

It is important to use a meaningful name for your project, so that you can easily find it at a later date. You can choose the project title as the filename, or use another name. Remember that Windows allows you to save files with long names, and that these can include spaces.

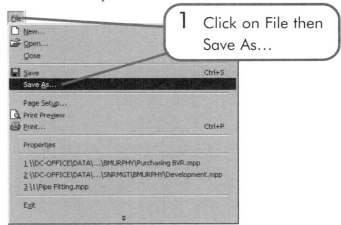

1 Click on File then Save As…

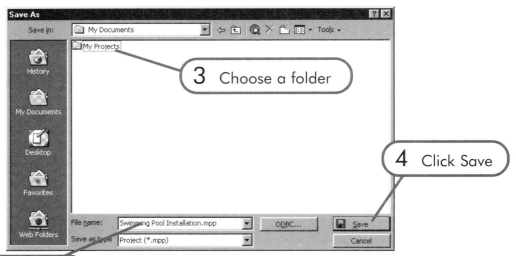

3 Choose a folder

4 Click Save

2 Give it a name

Save options

When you save your project file you can access a number of useful tools. These tools provide a more flexible method of securing your project file.

A protection password will stop unauthorised users from opening your project file. A Write reservation password allows others to open the project file, however they will be unable to make changes under your chosen project file name.

When you add some tasks (the actual work activities) to your project and then save, you have the option to save with a baseline. A baseline is a copy of your original project plan and it can be used later to compare planned against actual. This is discussed on page 72.

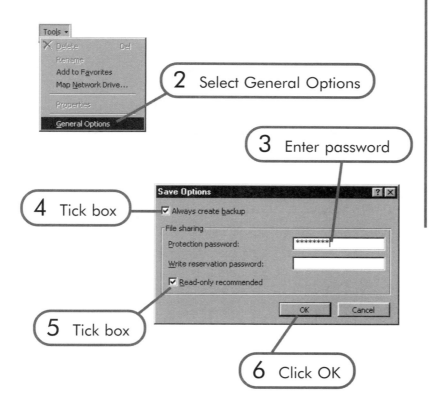

Basic steps

1 From the File menu, select Save As... then Tools.

2 Select General Options.

3 Add a password to your project file.

4 Tick the Always create backup checkbox to ensure that a backup file copy is taken each time you save your project.

5 Tick the Read-only recommended checkbox to ensure that your project file will not be accidentally changed by someone else.

6 Click OK.

7 Click Save.

6

The Gantt Chart view

Resources are the staff, plant, machinery and materials that are used to complete project tasks.

The default view for your project is the Gantt Chart view. This view allows you to look at the tasks that make up your project in a tabular and graphical format. The left side of your screen shows the tasks and the right side shows each task as bars on a timescale starting from the project start date you entered in Project Information.

Calendar

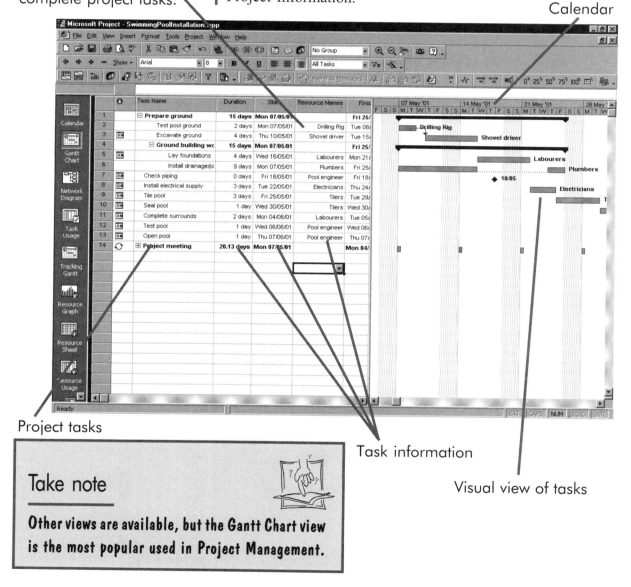

Project tasks

Task information

Visual view of tasks

Take note

Other views are available, but the Gantt Chart view is the most popular used in Project Management.

Adding tasks

All projects are made up of tasks, particular work items, measured in duration. They can often be split down into component tasks. Each has a name, duration, a start and finish date and has assigned to it some resources, i.e. materials measured in quantities or labour measured in time.

Take note

Project 2000 automatically assigns a sequential Task ID to each project task. This ID does not require that tasks be completed in the order listed.

Basic steps

1 Select the Task Name field and enter a suitable name for your task. Press [Return].

❑ Note that the duration of the task defaults to 1 day. (This is denoted by the question mark)

2 Repeat Step 1 for the remaining tasks in your project.

❑ Make task names descriptive so that they clearly define the task to be completed.

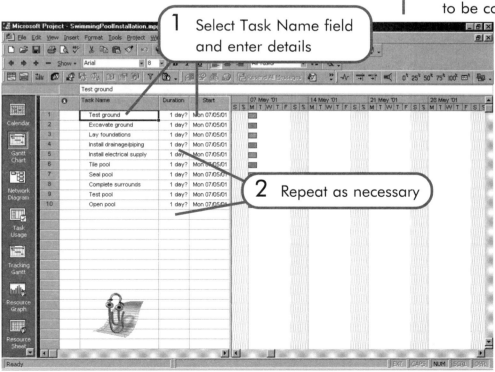

1 Select Task Name field and enter details

2 Repeat as necessary

Basic steps

1 From the Tools menu, select Options…

2 Click on the Calendar tab to review project calendar information.

3 Make any changes that are appropriate to your working week.

4 Click OK.

Project calendar

Each task takes a period of working time to complete. Depending on the way you've set your project up (on page 3) will determine the actual working hours in a week.

1 Select Tools then Options

2 Select Calendar

Take note

Project 2000 will assign task durations to work over the working times defined in the project calendar. This means that, under normal settings, project tasks will not be completed at weekends or in the evenings.

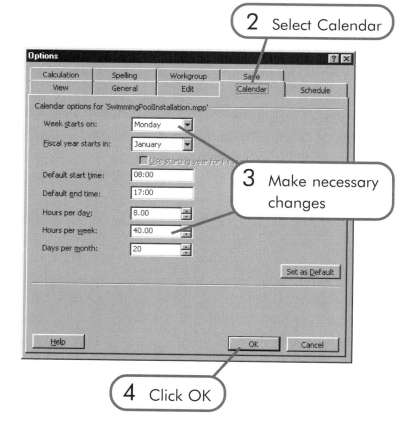

3 Make necessary changes

4 Click OK

Task durations

Project tasks can be entered in timescales that suit you. The following abbreviations are in place to make life easier for you. Use them to enter durations for each of the tasks in your project. Should the duration require the spanning of a time that is not included in your project calendar (e.g. a weekend or an evening) you can force the task to use non-working time by placing an 'e' (for 'evening') in front of the appropriate abbreviation for task duration. For example a 10-hour task that required to carry on into the evening would be entered as '10eh' rather than '10h'.

Abbreviation	Description
D	Day
W	Week
Mo	Month
M	Minute
H	Hour

Basic steps

1 Enter the task duration in the form '2d' or '4h' etc.

2 The Gantt Chart view will show the duration for each task as a bar.

3 Repeat steps 1-2 for all tasks.

❏ All your project tasks, start on the first date of your project, until or unless you set individual start dates.

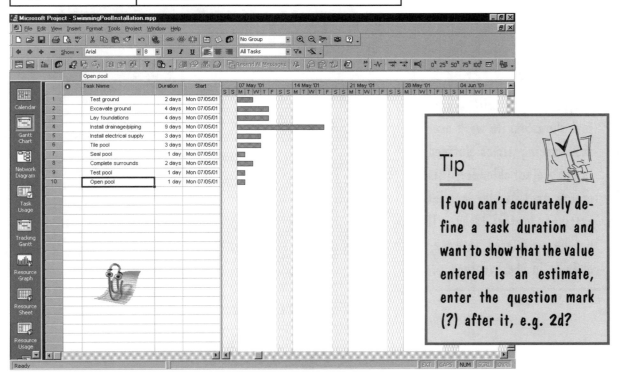

Tip

If you can't accurately define a task duration and want to show that the value entered is an estimate, enter the question mark (?) after it, e.g. 2d?

Basic steps

1 From the View bar, select the Gantt Chart view.

2 Click on a task to have notes added.

3 On the Standard toolbar, click on the Task Notes icon.

4 Enter notes as re-quired.

5 Click OK.

❑ The notes field allows extensive formatting to take place. Spend some time changing font size, alignment and even entering an image into the notes area for each task.

Task notes

Each task in your project can be associated with some notes. These allow you to add qualitative information to your task that is not recorded elsewhere. You might think of this area as a 'Post-it' board for your task.

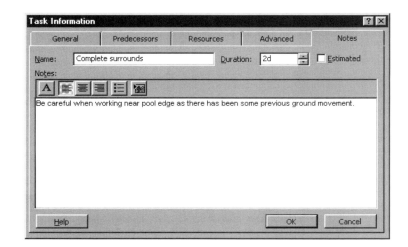

Take note

Notes can be added to resources and assignments as well as tasks.

Printing your project

Now that you've added some project tasks and durations you'll want to print out your project.

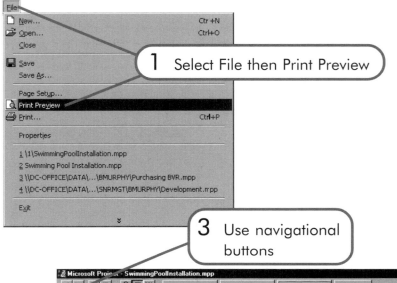

1 Select File then Print Preview

1 From the File menu, select Print Preview.

2 Preview your print.

3 Use the navigational buttons to view the complete report.

4 Use the Zoom, One Page and Multiple Pages icons to see different views.

5 Click Print…

Or

6 Click Close.

3 Use navigational buttons

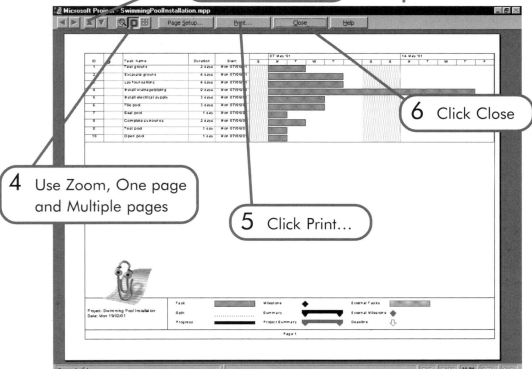

6 Click Close

4 Use Zoom, One page and Multiple pages

5 Click Print…

Basic steps

Closing Project 2000

❏ Setting Autosave

1 From the Tools menu, select Options.

2 Click on the Save tab.

3 In the AutoSave section, tick the 'Save every' check box and choose an appropriate time period between each save.

4 Click OK.

❏ Closing Project 2000

5 Open the File menu and choose Exit.

6 Save the current project file.

Once you've completed your work with a live project you must remember to close Project 2000 down. If you've not saved the current project, you'll be prompted to do this before the application will completely close. It might also be useful to set the AutoSave function at this stage. This will ensure that you are prompted to save your work periodically, avoiding loss should your computer crash or if there is a power failure.

2 Select Save tab

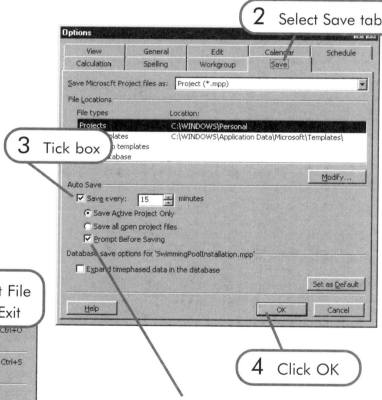

3 Tick box

4 Click OK

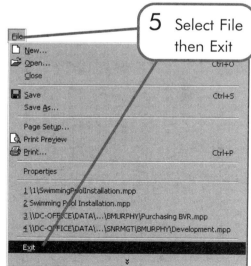

5 Select File then Exit

Tick the Prompt Before Saving checkbox to ensure that you don't automatically save an unwanted version of the project during an Autosave.

Summary

- ❏ Project 2000 forms part of Microsoft's Office 2000 suite of applications.

- ❏ Every project file has properties that allow you to record some scheduling detail about the project.

- ❏ A project is made up of a number of tasks. Each task takes a particular time to complete.

- ❏ Open Project 2000 by choosing Microsoft Project from the Start menu.

- ❏ Use New on the File menu to create a new project.

- ❏ Project properties allow you to record base project identifiaction information.

- ❏ Choose Save or Save As from the File menu to save your project.

- ❏ Views allow project information to be viewed in different formats.

- ❏ Calendars allow you to determine work patterns for your project.

- ❏ A task's duration is the time taken to complete that task.

- ❏ Task notes enable the recording of useful information against a project task.

- ❏ Choose Print Preview from the File menu to view and print your project details.

- ❏ Choose Exit from the File menu to close Project 2000.

2 Working with views

Project 2000 views 16

Calendar view 17

The Gantt Chart view 18

Changing the fiscal year 20

Network diagram view 21

Task usage view 22

Resource Usage view 23

Summary 24

Project 2000 views

Project 2000 provides you with many different ways of viewing project information to suit your requirements at the time, and to cater for the diverse information needs of the stakeholders in your project. Views are split into three broad categories:

Task views provide you with useful ways of viewing project tasks. Typically they include the Gantt Chart, Task Sheet and Task Usage views.

Resource views enable you to easily track resources used within your project. Resources are the staff, plant, machinery and materials that are used to complete project tasks. Project 2000 includes the Resource Graph, Resource Sheet and Resource Usage views.

Assignment views allow you to view the resources assigned to each task. The most common assignment views are the Task Usage and Resource Usage views.

Basic steps

1 Click on the View bar.

2 Click on a selection of available views.

3 Return to Gantt Chart view when complete.

Take note

Project data entered in one view is instantly available when you switch to another view.

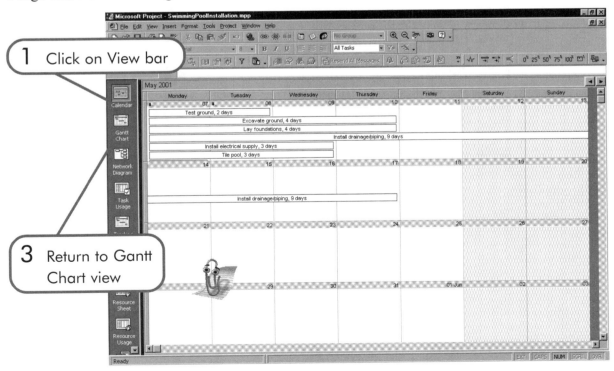

1 Click on View bar

3 Return to Gantt Chart view

Basic steps

1 Click on the Calendar icon from the View bar. (Note that four weeks of tasks are displayed.)

2 Use the arrow keys to move through the lifetime of your project.

3 From the File menu, select Print.

4 Choose the date range to be printed.

5 Click OK.

❑ Right-click on any task and the Task Information dialog box appears allowing you to change task names, resources and other task information.

❑ Pointing to the right edge of a task and dragging it to a new date changes the task duration.

Calendar view

The Calendar view provides you with a recognisable calendar showing each project task spanning a number of calendar days. It is suited to look at the weekly task schedule in a project and can be useful as a project wall chart. This view allows you to easily amend tasks by changing their duration.

1 Click Calendar

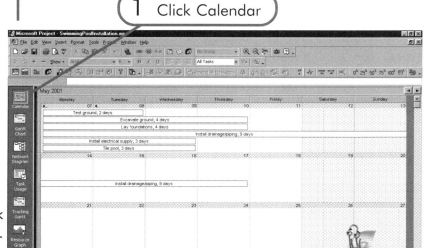

Tip

Double-click on a date to see all the tasks set for that date.

The Gantt Chart view

The Gantt Chart view offers you a great way to quickly see the sequence of project tasks on a timescale. This view also offers you a tabular task view, which allows you to easily add, amend and delete project tasks. You can easily format the output generated in this view.

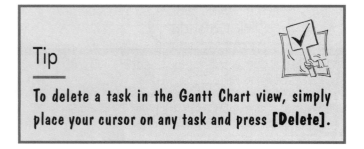

Tip

To delete a task in the Gantt Chart view, simply place your cursor on any task and press **[Delete]**.

Basic steps

1 Click on the Gantt Chart icon in the View bar.

2 Add or amend tasks as required in the table.

3 Use the navigational bars to move around the view.

4 Drag the windows to show more or less of the table/Gantt Chart.

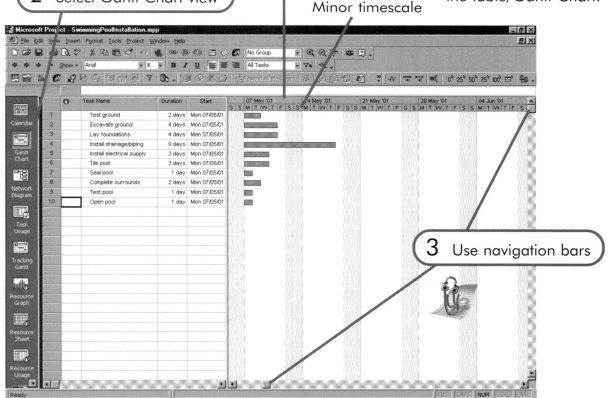

Major timescale

Minor timescale

2 Select Gantt Chart view

3 Use navigation bars

18

Basic steps

❑ Changing timescales

5 Click on the major timescale.

6 Right-click and choose Timescale…

7 Make changes to the major and minor timescales.

8 Check the preview.

9 Click OK.

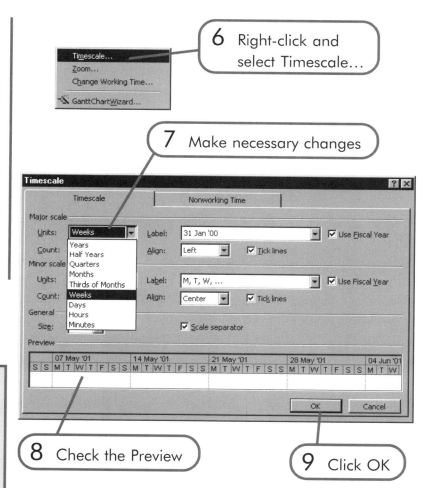

6 Right-click and select Timescale…

7 Make necessary changes

8 Check the Preview

9 Click OK

Tip

To move a task to a different position in the task list click on the ID column of the task to select it, then click once more on the ID column, hold the left mouse button down and drag to the new position.

Take note

Project 200 is a comprehensive project management tool that comes complete with many standard views as well as many more complex views of your project data. Spend some time looking through the views available on the View menu. Choose the More Views option for a list of further views.

Changing the fiscal year

Project 2000 allows you to change defaults to match your company's fiscal year. The fiscal year does not always run as the standard calendar year and this option allows you to include your own specific working method in projects.

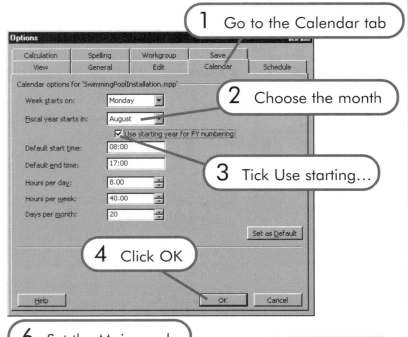

1 Go to the Calendar tab

2 Choose the month

3 Tick Use starting…

4 Click OK

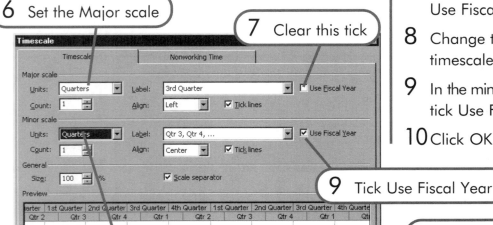

6 Set the Major scale

7 Clear this tick

8 Set the Minor scale

9 Tick Use Fiscal Year

10 Click OK

Basic steps

1 From the Tools menu, select Options… and go to the Calendar tab.

2 Choose a new month for the fiscal year.

3 Tick Use starting year for FY numbering.

4 Click OK.

5 Go to Gantt Chart view and double-click on the timescale displayed.

6 Change the major timescale to *Quarters*.

7 In the Major timescale remove the tick from Use Fiscal Year.

8 Change the Minor timescale to *Quarters*.

9 In the minor timescale tick Use Fiscal Year.

10 Click OK.

Network Diagram view

Basic steps

1 Click on the Network Diagram icon in the View menu.

2 Double-click on a node field.

3 Make any changes.

4 Click OK.

The Network Diagram view allows you to view your tasks and their dependencies in flowchart form. Many people still prefer to view project schedules this way.

In this view, tasks are commonly known as nodes. You can add, edit and amend tasks easily in this view by clicking in the appropriate task (node) and changes the appropriate field.

● Tasks started but not yet completed are shown with a single diagonal line through the node.

● Completed tasks have a crossed diagonal line.

● Tasks yet to start have no lines shown through them.

Tip

A single click on a node field will clear that field when you start typing. For non-destructive edits, double-click on the field.

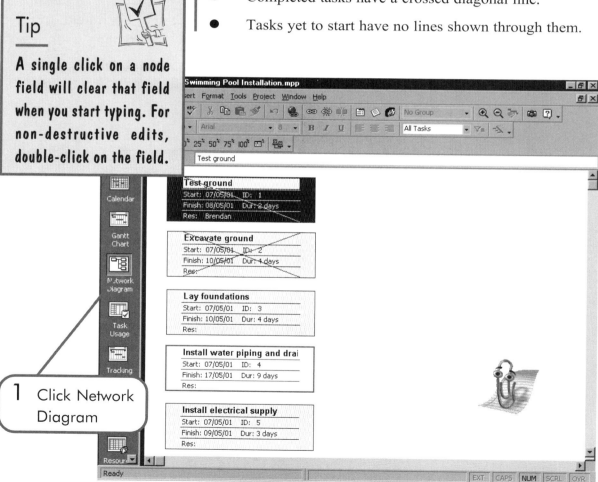

1 Click Network Diagram

Task usage view

The Task Usage view provides a great way to view the number of hours of work or cost each task requires in terms of resources used to complete it. You can use this view to track actual versus planned work.

> ## Take note
>
> For more about resources and assigning costs, see pages 44 and 66.

Basic steps

1 Click Task Usage.

2 Click on *Work* in the first task's Details.

3 Right-click for the shortcut menu and select Actual Work.

4 From the Format menu, select Detail Styles.

5 For each field, make formatting changes.

6 Click OK.

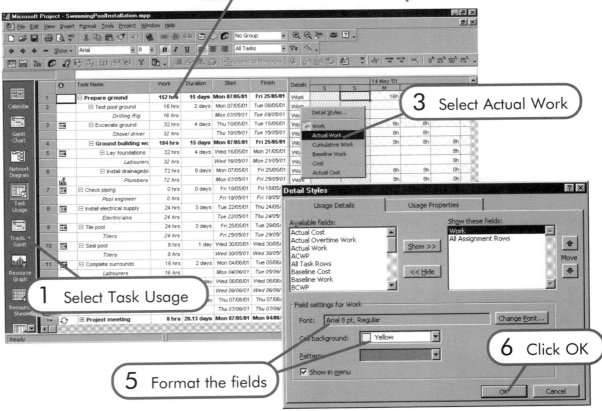

2 Click on Work

3 Select Actual Work

1 Select Task Usage

5 Format the fields

6 Click OK

Basic steps

1 From the View bar, click on the Resource Usage icon.

2 From the Format menu choose Details.

3 Choose appropriate fields to be included in the view.

Resource Usage view

The Resource Usage view allows you to track the tasks assigned to a particular resource and identify its total amount of work on each task. This is a great way of determining whether a particular resource has been assigned too much work during a particular time period.

From the **Details** menu item, add the *Overallocation* field to determine on a daily basis the amount of hours over normal work that a resource has been allocated. This lets you schedule extra resources or plan overtime for existing resources.

Take note

Resources are discussed later. This shows a project with resources already added.

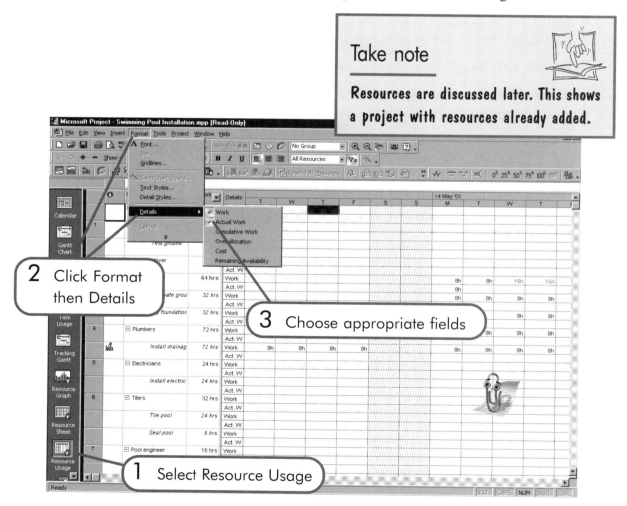

2 Click Format then Details

3 Choose appropriate fields

1 Select Resource Usage

Summary

❑ Project 2000 comes with over 20 views available.

❑ A view allows you to display project information in a variety of formats.

❑ The Calendar view shows your project in a recognisable calendar format.

❑ The Gantt Chart view shows project tasks in a combined tabular and bar format.

❑ The Fiscal Year reflects an organisation's accountancy year.

❑ The Network Diagram view shows project tasks in flowchart format.

❑ The Task Usage view allows you to view allocated work hours against project tasks.

❑ The Resource Usage view allows you to view tasks against project resources.

❑ Project 2000 includes a wide range of other views that can be used in the management of your project.

3 Getting Help

Using Help 26

The Help index 27

Screen tips 28

Using Office Assistant 29

Project Help on the Web 30

Wizards 31

Summary 32

Using Help

Project 2000 comes with a very comprehensive system of Help that should answer almost every question you have about the software, and about project management in general. From the moment you start the package, Help is provided in the form of a window covering the right-hand portion of your screen. From here, you can find out about new features included in the current version of the software, take a quick tour, look at a detailed discussion on project management skills, and have access to a wide source of referenced Help.

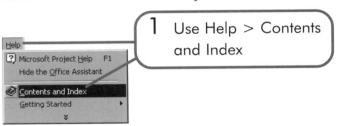

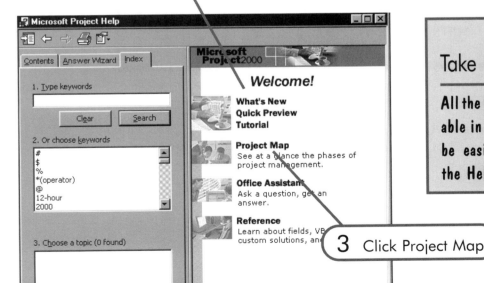

Basic steps

1 From the Help menu, select Contents and Index.

2 Click on Quick Preview and take a quick tour of Project 2000.

3 Click on Project Map and find out great information on the basics of effective project management.

4 Take some time to have a look around the other Help resources provided.

5 Close the Help index.

Take note

All the Help options available in Project 2000 can be easily accessed from the Help menu.

Basic steps

1 From the Help menu, select Contents and Index.

2 Type in the word you want to search for.

3 Click Search.

4 Choose from the Help topics listed.

5 Click on the Print icon to print the topic.

6 Click on the Back icon to look through previous Help topic pages.

7 Click on the Clear button to start a new search.

8 Close the Help index.

The Help index

Project 2000 comes with the traditional Help index found in most Windows applications. Here, you can enter in a keyword and choose a topic to further explore.

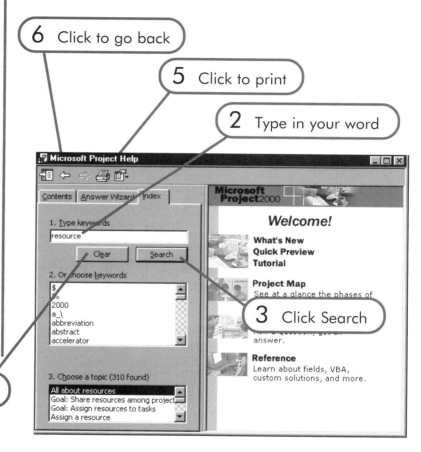

6 Click to go back

5 Click to print

2 Type in your word

3 Click Search

7 Click Clear

Tip

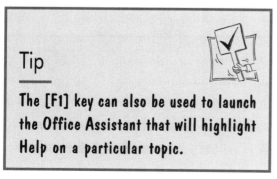

The [F1] key can also be used to launch the Office Assistant that will highlight Help on a particular topic.

ScreenTips

Project 2000 allows you to access instant Help by simply hovering your mouse over the area of interest. You are then offered fairly detailed information. Hover over tasks, and summary information is provided. Hovering over screen elements such as a column heading, allows you to access further hypertext Help on that item.

A hypertext link is a word or group of words that, when clicked, link to a further source of information. Hypertext links are often available in Help screens and are a basic feature of Web pages. Images can also act as links to other sources of information.

Basic steps

1 Click on the Gantt Chart view in the View bar.

2 Place your mouse over one of the bars on the Gantt chart.

3 Note the underlying task information.

4 Hover over a column heading.

5 Click on the hyperlink for more information.

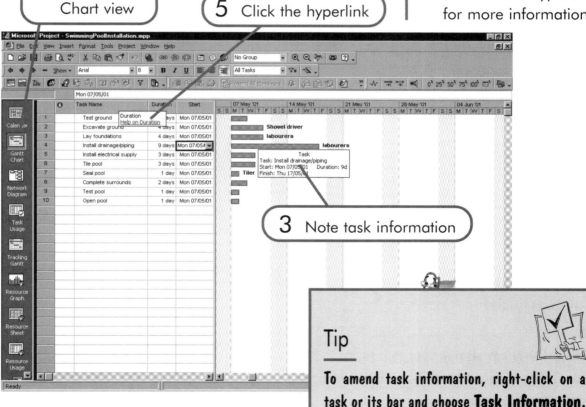

1 Click Gantt Chart view

5 Click the hyperlink

3 Note task information

Tip

To amend task information, right-click on a task or its bar and choose **Task Information**.

Basic steps

1 Click on the Office Assistant image.

2 Key in a question.

3 Click Search.

❑ To change the appearance of Office Assistant

4 Right-click on the Office Assistant and choose Options...

5 Open the Gallery tab.

6 Use Back and Next to choose from the available assistants.

7 Open the Options tab.

8 Adjust the way that the Assistant works, then click OK.

Using Office Assistant

The Microsoft Office Assistant will be familiar to you if you use other Office 2000 family products. The Office Assistant is an intelligent Help tool that will offer Help tips and allow you to ask questions and receive answers. In this version of the software, the default Office Assistant is a dinky little cartoon paperclip with a face!

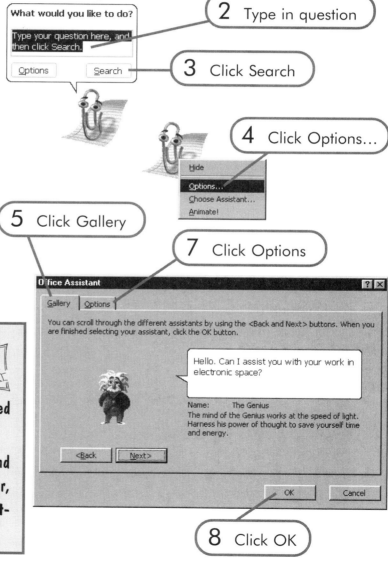

What would you like to do?

Type your question here, and then click Search.

Options   Search

2 Type in question

3 Click Search

4 Click Options...

Hide
Options...
Choose Assistant...
Animate!

5 Click Gallery

7 Click Options

Office Assistant   ? ×

Gallery | Options

You can scroll through the different assistants by using the <Back and Next> buttons. When you are finished selecting your assistant, click the OK button.

Hello. Can I assist you with your work in electronic space?

Name: The Genius
The mind of the Genius works at the speed of light. Harness his power of thought to save yourself time and energy.

<Back   Next>

OK   Cancel

8 Click OK

Tip

The Office Assistant can be dragged to any position on the screen.

To hide it, right-click on it, and choose 'Hide'. To make it reappear, choose Show the Office Assistant from the Help menu.

Project Help on the Web

For the most up-to-date application Help and information you must turn to the Web. Here, you can access great information and download software fixes and other useful project management information articles and advice direct from Microsoft.

Web Help can be accessed via the Help menu or through your browser by entering the following address:

www.microsoft.com/office/project/

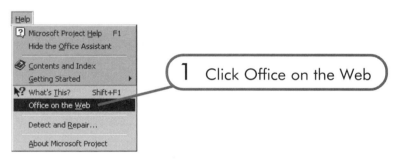

1 Click Office on the Web

Basic steps

1 From the Help menu choose the Office on the Web hyperlink.

2 Choose the appropriate country from the Office Update site.

3 Browse the available Help.

Take note

You must be on-line before using Web help.

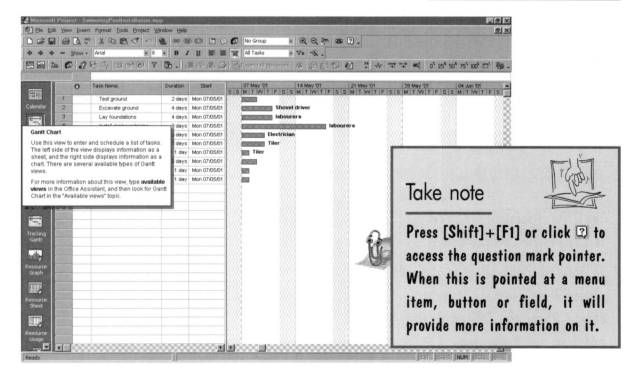

Take note

Press [Shift]+[F1] or click ⑦ to access the question mark pointer. When this is pointed at a menu item, button or field, it will provide more information on it.

Basic steps

1 From the Format menu, choose GanttChartWizard...

2 Make choices on the questions posed.

3 Click on the Format It button and watch your Gantt Chart be reformatted to suit your needs.

Project 2000, in keeping with the Office 2000 family, provides wizards to Help you through common tasks. The Office Assistant is used in Project 2000 to help with wizards such as the GanttChartWizard, found in the Format menu.

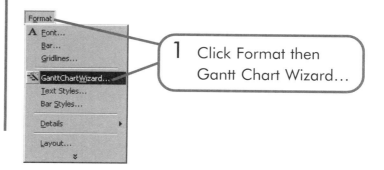

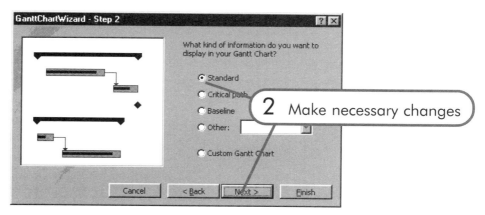

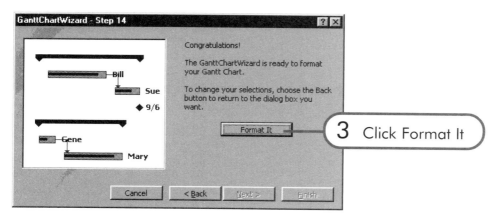

Summary

❏ Project 2000 has a comprehensive Help system that enables you to find out about the software as well as about general project management principles.

❏ [F1] invokes the Office Assistant.

❏ Screen Tips are widely available.

❏ The Office Assistant allow you to enter a question and have it answered.

❏ Help is available from the Microsoft Web site.

❏ Use [Shift]-[F1] for point-and-click Help.

❏ Use wizards to guide you through Project 2000 processes.

4 Project building blocks

Project objectives 34

Creating a task list 35

Recurring tasks 36

Summary tasks 37

Outlining a task list 38

Outline numbering 39

Splitting tasks 40

The critical path 41

Summary 42

Project objectives

It is important from the outset to have a clear view of the purpose of a project. Clear objectives are needed to effectively manage projects that incur costs, resources and take time to complete. Essentially, planning of objectives must be completed at the start of any project.

Objectives should:

- be clear and achievable;

- define project 'deliverables', i.e. the final products or services;

- define any budgets in terms of cost, resources and time;

- be communicated to all project stakeholders.

Good communication is at the essence of effective project management. Problems and difficulties are easier to manage, and contingencies worked out, the earlier accurate information can be provided. Regular project meetings are a great aid to communication.

It is also important at the outset to determine the project scope. This will help keep focus on the business of the project and reduce the chance of becoming distracted.

All projects will start with some assumptions. These should be clearly listed and should be reviewed regularly to determine their continued relevance. Similarly, any constraints that exist must be identified. A typical constraint might be that the project must be finished by a certain date.

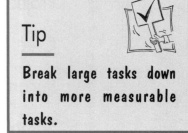

Tip

Break large tasks down into more measurable tasks.

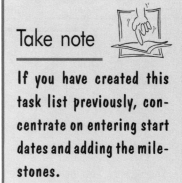

Take note

If you have created this task list previously, concentrate on entering start dates and adding the milestones.

Basic steps

1 Select Gantt Chart view.

2 Enter the name in the Task Name field and give it a Duration.

3 Enter a Start date.

4 Continue as above until you've created a comprehensive project task list.

5 Create a milestone task by assigning it a duration of 0d. The Gantt Chart shows this with a black diamond.

Creating a task list

A task list identifies the tasks required to complete your project. Each task should result in a deliverable and tasks should be small enough in length to be easily tracked and managed. A milestone is a special task that identifies a major point in the life of your project. A milestone might be the completion of a particular phase of the project or the delivery of a particular product or service.

1 Click Gantt Chart view

Milestone

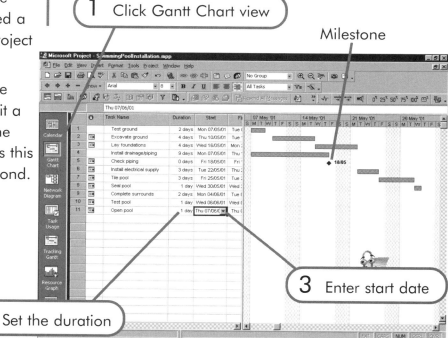

2 Set the duration

3 Enter start date

Take note

Any task in your project can act as a milestone. To make one a milestone, right-click on it and on the Advanced tab in the Task Information dialog box, check the 'Mark task a milestone' checkbox. You can also set a deadline on this tab.

Recurring tasks

A regular project meeting, maybe held weekly, is a good example of a 'recurring task'.

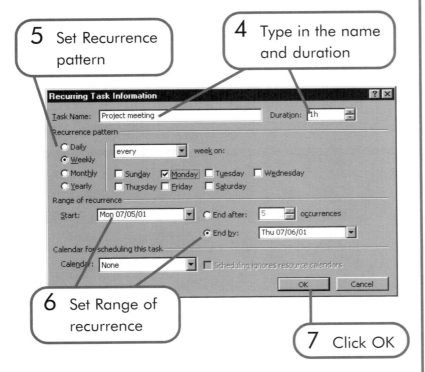

5 Set Recurrence pattern

4 Type in the name and duration

6 Set Range of recurrence

7 Click OK

1 From the View bar select Gantt Chart view.

2 Click on the space below the last task in your project.

3 From the Insert menu, choose Recurring task...

4 Give your recurring task a suitable name and duration.

5 Choose the Recurrence pattern, including a particular weekday.

6 Set the Range of the recurrence in terms of the number of times or select the End by date.

7 Click OK.

Tip

To view all the occurrences of a recurring task, click on the '+' sign in the top left-hand corner of the recurring task's name. Click again to hide these occurrences.

Hide/Show recurring tasks

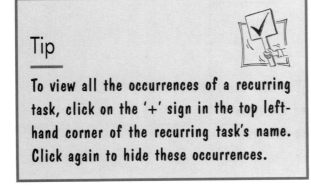

14	↻	⊟ Project meeting	20.13 days	Mon 07/05/01	Mon 04/06/01
15	▦	Project meeting 1	1 hr	Mon 07/05/01	Mon 07/05/01
16	▦	Project meeting 2	1 hr	Mon 14/05/01	Mon 14/05/01
17	▦	Project meeting 3	1 hr	Mon 21/05/01	Mon 21/05/01
18	▦	Project meeting 4	1 hr	Mon 28/05/01	Mon 28/05/01
19	▦	Project meeting 5	1 hr	Mon 04/06/01	Mon 04/06/01

Basic steps

1 Click on the task below where the summary task is to go.

2 From the Insert menu, choose New Task.

3 Give your summary task a suitable name.

4 Click on the first task below the summary that will be part of it.

5 From the Standard toolbar, click on the Indent icon.

6 Repeat steps 4–5 for each sub-task.

❑ Summary tasks are shown in bold in table views and on Gantt Charts as thick black lines.

Tip

If you indent a task without creating a summary task above it, Project 2000 makes the previous task the summary task.

Summary tasks allow you to group a set of related tasks in order to view them as one main task. A summary task is not the same as a normal task in the sense that it cannot be edited in terms of its start date or duration. Its duration is automatically calculated by taking the earliest and last date from the tasks that make it up, termed 'sub-tasks'. Summary tasks are useful for giving a broad overview of your project.

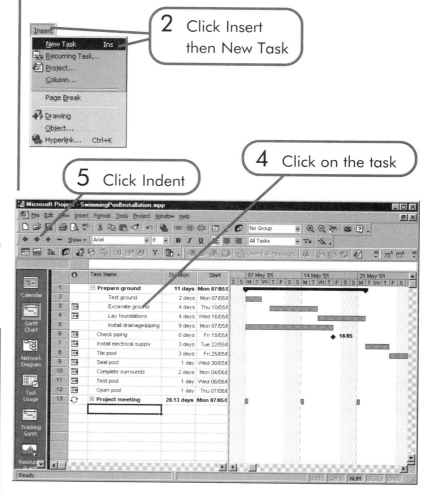

2 Click Insert then New Task

4 Click on the task

5 Click Indent

Outlining a task list

Outlining tasks enables you to effectively manage your project in terms of creating summary tasks and sub-tasks beneath them. This makes it easy to see relationships within the tasks in your project. You can then choose to view only summary tasks in the Gantt Chart view.

● Recurring tasks are shown, even when a summary task view is requested.

Sub-tasks can also be summary tasks, and have their own sets of sub-tasks.

❑ Viewing only summary tasks

1 Ensure that the Gantt Chart view is selected.

2 On the Formatting toolbar click the Filter drop-down list box.

3 Select Summary Tasks.

❑ Creating summary tasks from sub-tasks

4 Click on the sub-task.

5 From the Insert menu choose New Task.

6 Name the new task.

7 Click on each task to become part of this summary and indent as appropriate.

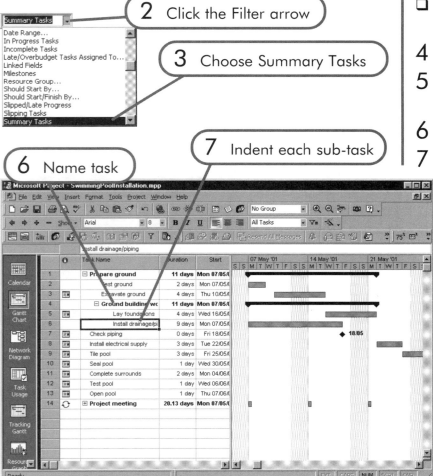

2 Click the Filter arrow

3 Choose Summary Tasks

6 Name task

7 Indent each sub-task

Tip

To add a new task go to the task below where the new task is to be shown and press [Insert].

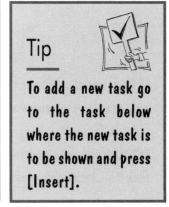

Basic steps

1 From the Tools menu, select Options.

2 Click on the View tab.

3 Tick the Show outline number checkbox.

4 Click OK.

Outline numbering

Project 2000 provides you with a great means of automatically numbering tasks with a recognised pattern of numbers. This is sometimes useful if your project has many tasks and sub-tasks as it gives you another common way of referencing project tasks.

2 Open the View tab

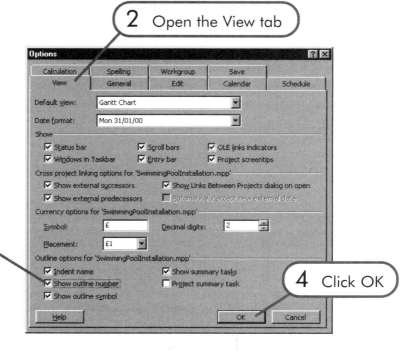

3 Tick Show outline number

4 Click OK

Take note

Custom outline codes are generated by you, and they can also be used to provide structure to tasks and resources. These codes are often used for accountancy purposes or job-costing purposes. More information can be found using the Office Assistant Help.

Outline numbering

	ⓘ	Task Name	Duration	Start	
1		⊟ 1 Prepare ground	11 days	Mon 07/05/01	Mo
2		1.1 Test pool ground	2 days	Mon 07/05/01	Tu
3	🖼	1.2 Excavate ground	4 days	Thu 10/05/01	Tu
4		⊟ 1.3 Ground building	11 days	Mon 07/05/01	Mo
5	🖼	1.3.1 Lay foundat	4 days	Wed 16/05/01	Mo
6		1.3.2 Install drains	9 days	Mon 07/05/01	Th
7	🖼	2 Check piping	0 days	Fri 18/05/01	F

39

Splitting tasks

Some tasks may be split between two time periods in your project rather than occur in a straightforward time sequence. An example might be that the installation of piping for the pool needs to be completed just before the pool is tested. Project 2000 allows you to split project tasks.

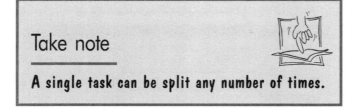

Take note

A single task can be split any number of times.

3 Click Split

1 From the View bar, select Gantt Chart view.

2 Select the task.

3 Click the Split Task icon.

4 In the right-hand pane click on the date that the task is to be split.

5 Click on the remainder of the task and drag it to the date for work on the task to resume.

To remove a split, click on the split portion and drag it back to the previous part of the task bar.

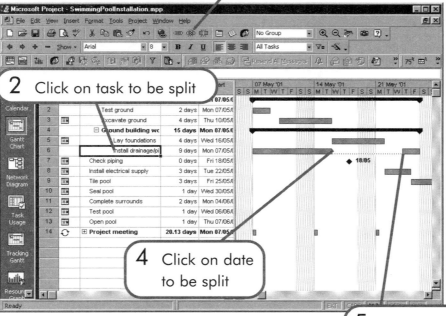

2 Click on task to be split

4 Click on date to be split

5 Set date to resume task

The critical path

Every project you work with will have a critical path. The critical path is the list of tasks in the project that dictate the finish date of the project. If any of the tasks in the critical path (the critical tasks) are delayed or are extended in any way then the project cannot finish on time.

A critical task is a task that, if it is delayed, has an overall effect on the finish time of your project. In Project 2000 a task is critical if it has no slack, if it has a *Must Start On* or *Must Finish On* constraint. Projects scheduled from a start date will also throw up critical tasks where an *As Late As Possible* constraint is evident and on projects where scheduling is from a finish date, an *As Soon As Possible* constraint will make a task critical. A task is also deemed critical if it has a finish date that is equal to or extends beyond its deadline date (if one has been entered).

You can view the critical path for your project easily, using the Detail Gantt view, found in the More Views area of the View bar.

Take note

If your project is time-critical then it is essential that you keep a very keen eye on the project's critical path to ensure that critical tasks are completed on time.

Take note

Once a critical task has been completed, it stops being critical, as it can then have no effect on the rest of the project.

Summary

- ❑ Before you start a new project, it is essential that you have a clear understanding of the purpose of it.

- ❑ Define project tasks in a task list.

- ❑ A milestone is a major completion point in a project.

- ❑ Recurring tasks are tasks that repeat during the lifetime of a project.

- ❑ A summary task allows you to group a set of related tasks.

- ❑ Outlining a list of tasks allows you to create summary tasks spanning the duration of the task list.

- ❑ Outline numbering allows you to create custom sequential numbers to project tasks.

- ❑ Split tasks allow tasks to be part-completed, put on hold, then continued at a later date.

- ❑ The critical path is the name given to the sequence of tasks that must be finished on time to ensure the project keeps to its deadline.

5 Managing resources

What are project resources? 44

Creating a resource list 45

Using a resource pool 47

Changing your calendar 49

Multiple-base calendars 50

Project assignments 51

Resource levelling 54

Summary 56

Project resources

Project resources are the resources required to successfully complete a project and deliver some product or service. The most obvious project resource are people. People are needed to carry out most of the tasks in a typical project. However apart from people, other resources could include machinery, plant or equipment required to carry out tasks as well as the material required to carry out tasks that require something to be produced – such as the bricks and mortar used in the construction of a wall.

Project 2000 considers resources to be either work resources or material resources. Work resources include people, machinery and equipment as these are used to perform a function to complete a task. These resources are normally measured in terms of the time required to work on each task. Material resources are those supplies or consumable items required to complete a particular task and are measured in quantities.

Resources allow you to exercise control over your project in terms of time and costs. They allow you to clearly identify responsibility in terms of tasks required to be completed and this allows you to manage effectively the people, machinery, equipment and material at your disposal. Use of resources in terms of people allows you to determine workload, ensuring that project staff are being fully utilised.

Work resources can be people, mentioned by name, or they can be people mentioned by job title or generic job function or skill.

Material resources can be material mentioned by quantity used, or by the technical name of the material.

Basic steps

1 From the View bar, choose Resource Sheet.

2 In the Resource Name field, type a name.

3 Set the Type as a work or material resource.

4 In the Material Label field enter the unit of measurement for a material resource.

5 In Initials you can enter an abbreviation for the resource name – use ones that you will remember.

6 The Group field lets you group resources by type, for example, by department.

7 Enter hourly rates in the Std. Rate and Ovt. Rate to get costings.

❑ Repeat steps 2-7 for your project resources.

Creating a resource list

Resources can be used in a number of ways. First, a resource list can be set up when resources are being used solely within a single project. Once created, resources can then be allocated to tasks from a drop-down selection list. For a situation where more than one project is involved, see page 116.

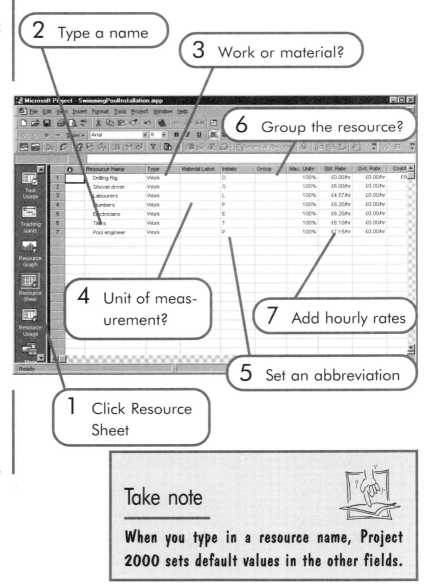

2 Type a name

3 Work or material?

6 Group the resource?

4 Unit of measurement?

7 Add hourly rates

5 Set an abbreviation

1 Click Resource Sheet

Take note

When you type in a resource name, Project 2000 sets default values in the other fields.

Using resource lists from different projects

Project 2000 allows you to use the resource list created in another project for the current one. This could be useful when the total available resources are working between two projects.

Pool takes precedence should be used if you want the project *donating* the resources to take precedence in the event of a conflict. **Sharer takes precedence** should be chosen if the project *requesting* the shared resources should take precedence.

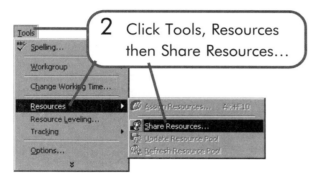

2 Click Tools, Resources then Share Resources...

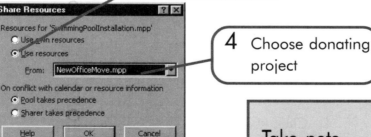

3 Tick Use resources

4 Choose donating project

6 Click OK

Basic steps

1 From the File menu, open the projects donating and receiving the resources.

2 From the Tools menu, choose Resources, then Share Resources...

3 Click Use resources.

4 Choose the donating project from the drop-down From: list.

5 If resource-sharing causes conflict in terms of overuse, then decide which should take precedence.

6 Click OK.

Take note

The Max. Units field lets you set the percentage of time that the resource can work on a task. For example, setting a resource's max. units to 70% will let you know that it can only work on the project task for 70% of its available work time.

Basic steps

Using a resource pool

1 From the File menu, open all the projects that need to share resources.

2 From the View bar, select Resource Sheet.

3 From the Project menu, select Project Information. Note the start or finish dates for each project depending on how you decided to schedule them.

4 Click the New icon.

5 Enter a start or finish date for the resource pool, then click OK.

A resource pool allows you to share resources among a number of projects that are being completed around the same dates.

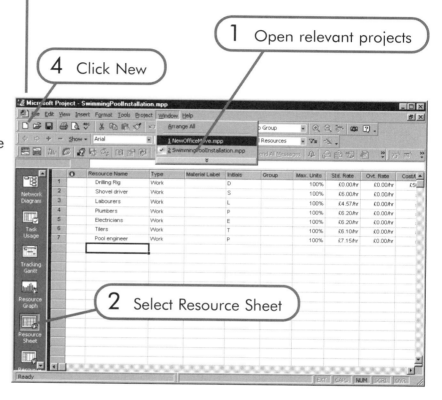

1 Open relevant projects

4 Click New

2 Select Resource Sheet

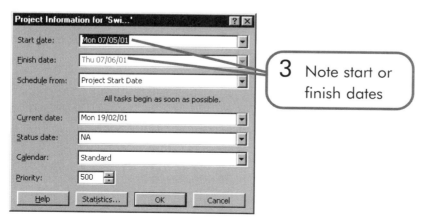

3 Note start or finish dates

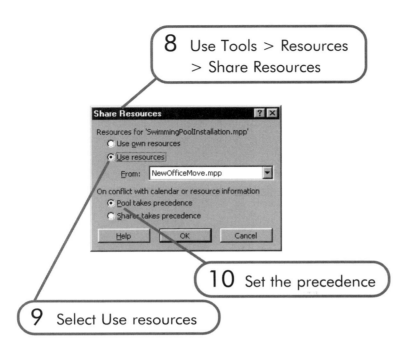

8 Use Tools > Resources > Share Resources

9 Select Use resources

10 Set the precedence

6 Select the folder to hold the new resource pool, give it a name and save it.

7 From the Window menu, select the first project whose resources are to be moved to the pool.

8 From the Tools menu, select Resources, then Share Resources.

9 Select Use resources and choose the resource pool file in the From: field.

10 Decide on resource sharing precedence and click OK.

❑ Repeat steps 7–10, then from the Window menu select the resource pool and click on Save.

Tip

When sharing requires information from a resource pool it's always better to make amendments in terms of hourly rates, etc. to the main pool, rather than have the receiving project overwrite these values. This make project control much easier to maintain.

Basic steps

1 From the Tools menu, select Change Working Times…

2 In the For: field, choose the calendar.

3 Select the dates, by selecting the first, then holding down [Shift] and selecting the final date in the range.

4 Set the Nondefault working times by entering working times in the available fields.

5 Enter any Nonworking dates.

6 Click OK.

Take note

The project base calendar defaults to Mon–Fri, 9–5 with one hour for lunch. Other base calendars (24 hours and night shift) are available.

Changing your calendar

Each project can have a number of calendars associated with it. These determine the way in which work resources* can be used within a project. The most common use is to set daily working times, holiday patterns, etc. Every project has a base calendar.

The project calendar, by default, is the project's base calendar and it's here that you can affect the schedule of resources.

Material resources are assumed to be available at all times.

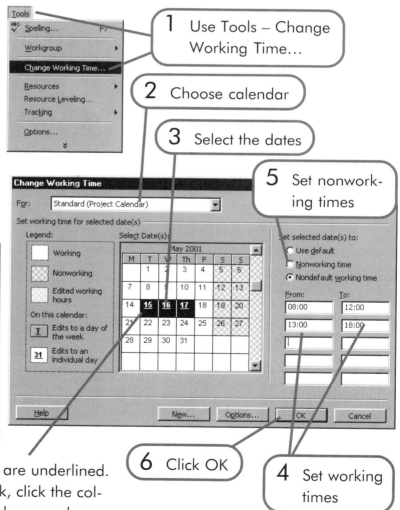

1 Use Tools – Change Working Time…

2 Choose calendar

3 Select the dates

5 Set nonworking times

6 Click OK

4 Set working times

Dates affected by changes are underlined. To adjust a day of the week, click the column day identifier then make your changes.

Multiple-base calendars

Multiple-base calendars are very useful for managing resources that don't operate on a standard shift basis. Typical examples might be part-time workers, those that work weekends only or those working split-shift rotas. Creating base calendars for each of these resources will make it easy to correctly assign and monitor workload.

1 From the Tools menu, select Change Working Time.

2 Click on the New… button.

3 Give the new base calendar a name.

4 Choose whether to create the calendar as a completely new entity or copy details from an existing calendar.

5 Click OK.

6 Make appropriate changes to the new calendar days/dates.

7 Click OK.

6 Make the changes

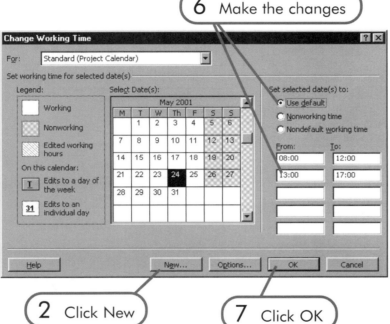

2 Click New

7 Click OK

3 Enter a name

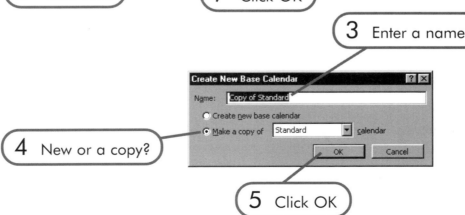

4 New or a copy?

5 Click OK

Basic steps

1 From the View bar, choose Gantt Chart view.

2 Click on the Resource Names field for the first task.

3 Use the drop-down list to choose a resource to assign to the task.

4 Repeat steps 2 - 3 for other tasks in your project.

Project assignments

Now that you have successfully created a project resource list and defined the work profile of resources in it, you can assign these resources to tasks in your project. This will allow you to keep a check on who or what is actually working on a particular task at a given time in the life of your project, thus aiding the management of it and of your resources.

Tip

If you need a resource that's not listed, jump back to the Resource Sheet view and add it.

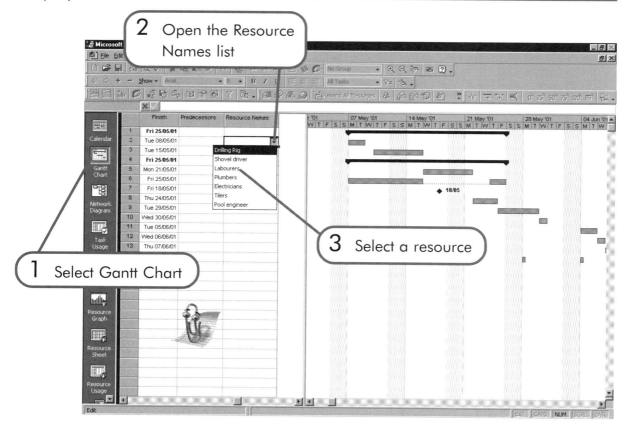

2 Open the Resource Names list

3 Select a resource

1 Select Gantt Chart

Assigning resources to a calendar

A particular resource can easily be assigned to a non-default base calendar.

A project can have a number of calendars associated with it. The base calendar is set when you create a new project and shows the working and non-working times for all resources in the project. The base calendar can also be the project calendar or the project calendar can be created from scratch. The project calendar holds the default working times for a particular project. The resource calendar(s) can be used to set working times for individual project resources.

1 From the View bar, select Resource Sheet view.

2 Select the resource to be amended.

3 Drop-down the Base Calendar list.

4 Select the calendar to use.

Accrue At = options for charging costs

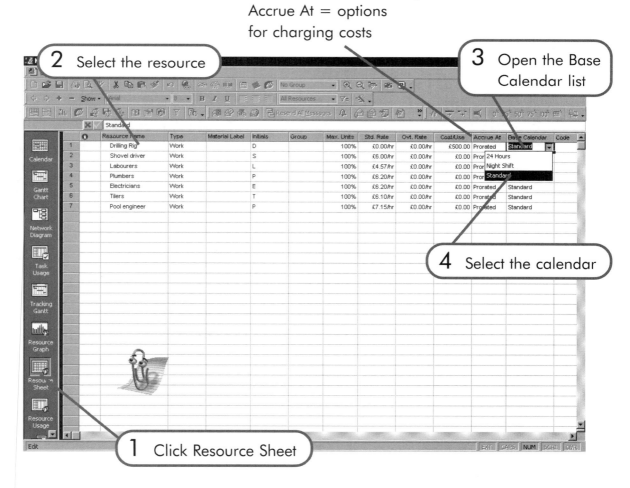

2 Select the resource

3 Open the Base Calendar list

4 Select the calendar

1 Click Resource Sheet

52

Assigning multiple resources to a task

1 Select the Gantt Chart view.

2 Click on a task to have resources added.

3 Move to the Resource Name field.

4 From the Standard toolbar, click on the Assign Resources icon.

5 Choose the resource.

6 Set the percentage involvement.

7 Click Assign.

❑ To remove a resource, call up the Assign Resources dialog box, select the resource and click Remove.

Some tasks will require more than one individual or skill to complete, and so must be associated with more than one resource. Project 2000 allows you to add multiple resources, splitting their time by the percentage used to complete the task.

When you add multiple resources to a task, its duration will change, as more resources should reduce its completion time. This type of scheduling is common and is said to be 'effort driven scheduling' and it is the default method used in Project 2000. If a task took 18 hours to complete, an allocation of 100% for one resource and 50% for a second would result in the first resource putting in 12 hours' and the second, 6 hours' effort.

Project 2000 uses this formula to calculate work to be complete:

Duration x Units = Work

where *Duration* is the time, *Units* are the resources used (and their percentage contribution to the task) and *Work* is the effort required to complete the task.

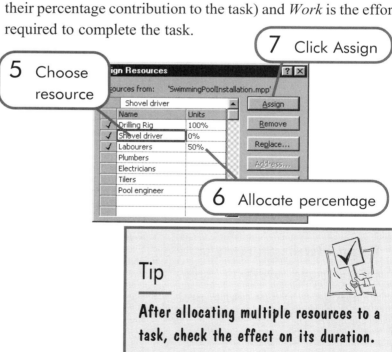

Tip

Use the Task Entry view to gain a better visual under-standing of the work breakdown for tasks using multiple resources.

Tip

After allocating multiple resources to a task, check the effect on its duration.

Resource levelling

Resource levelling is useful when a particular resource, usually a person, has been allocated project tasks that take up more time in a day than the number of working hours available for that resource.

Project 2000 allows you to easily sort out over-allocations by moving project tasks to accommodate the levelling.

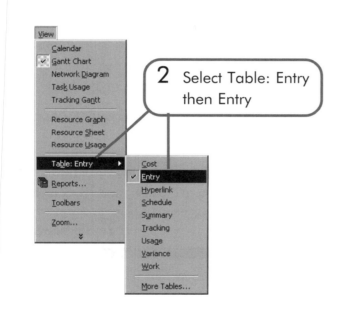

1 From the View bar, select Resource Sheet view.

2 From the View menu select Table: Entry then Entry.

❑ Note the over-allocated resources.

3 From the Tools menu, select Resource Levelling.

4 Choose to level manually.

5 Select the Day by Day option to fix over-allocations on a daily basis.

6 Click on Level entire project.

Take note

Resource leveling will almost certainly move project tasks. Remember to review your project after carrying it out.

Tip

Resources that are over-allocated are displayed in red in resource views.

7 Ensure that your Re-
source Leveling dialog
box matches the one
on the screen.

8 Click Level Now.

9 Click OK .

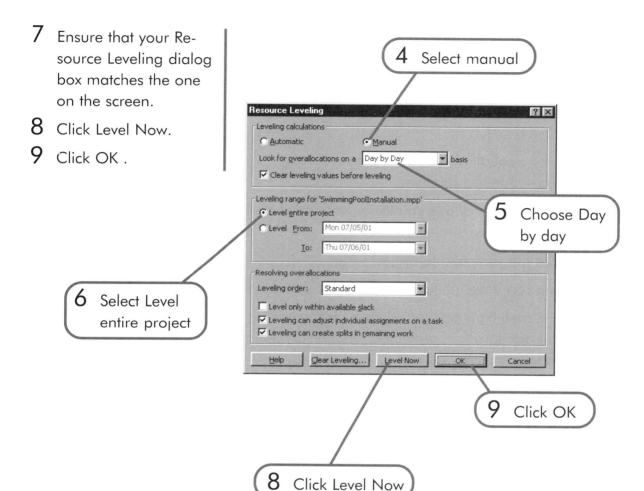

4 Select manual

5 Choose Day
by day

6 Select Level
entire project

9 Click OK

8 Click Level Now

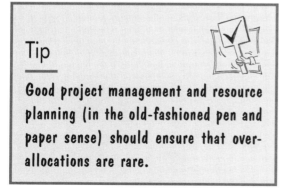

Tip

Good project management and resource
planning (in the old-fashioned pen and
paper sense) should ensure that over-
allocations are rare.

Summary

❑ Project resources are the people, machinery, materials and equipment needed to complete project tasks.

❑ A project resource list is a list of resources used in your project.

❑ A resource pool allows you to share resources among a number of projects.

❑ A project calendar allows you to set work times and shift patterns for each resource.

❑ Resources are assigned to project tasks.

❑ Each task can have multiple resources assigned to it.

❑ Resource levelling is applied when a resource is allocated more work in a day than that resource has the time to complete.

6 Linking tasks

Linking tasks 58

Different task links 59

Lag and lead times 60

Constraints 62

Summary 64

Linking tasks

As you work through a project, the likelihood is that certain tasks will be dependent on the completion of other tasks. For example, in a new house project, painting an interior wall will be dependent on that wall being first built and then plastered.

Linking tasks is very important as it is highly unlikely that any project will not require this method of task association, and it is easily done in Project 2000.

The benefit are:

● If a particular task is finished late, it's easy to see the effect this has on dependent tasks;

● You can have a graphic view of the relationship between tasks;

● Better task management.

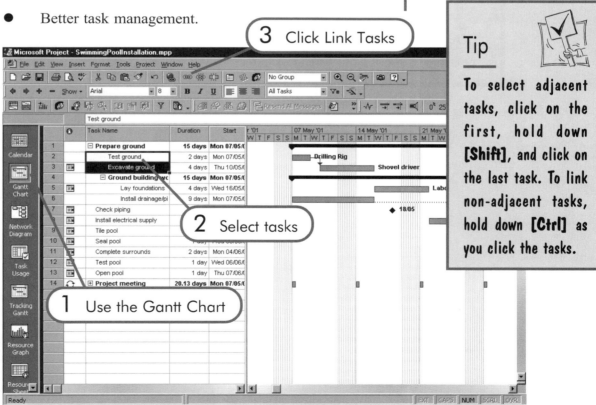

3 Click Link Tasks

2 Select tasks

1 Use the Gantt Chart

Tip

To select adjacent tasks, click on the first, hold down **[Shift]**, and click on the last task. To link non-adjacent tasks, hold down **[Ctrl]** as you click the tasks.

58

Different task links

1 Go to Gantt Chart view.

2 Choose two tasks to link.

3 Click the Link Tasks icon.

4 Double-click on the arrow linking the tasks.

5 Change the task dependency type.

6 Click OK.

In the above example, Project 2000 created 'finish to start' (FS) links where each task to be linked cannot start until the previous task is complete. Project 2000 provides other task dependency links.

● *Start to start* link (SS). This link is used when a particular task cannot start until another has started. An example might be 'demolish building' and 'clear rubble'.

● *Finish to finish* link (FF). This link is used where a particular task cannot finish until another is complete. An example might be 'Install lighting' and 'test lighting'.

● *Start to finish* link (SF). This is used when a particular task cannot finish until a previous one starts. An example might be that the milestone 'deliver conservatory' can't be complete until 'construct conservatory' is started.

Tip

To delete a task link, double-click on it, and click Delete.

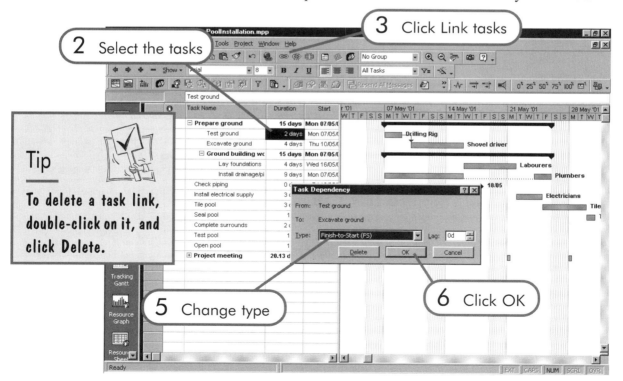

Lag and lead times

Lag times and lead times are useful when a task and a dependent task have a break between them. Lag time is a delay between one task finishing and another task beginning. Lead time is an overlap between dependent tasks. For example a lead time might allow a second task to start mid-way through the first task being completed.

When entering lag times, the values for task duration are always positive while lead time values are negative.

Basic steps

1 Go to the Gantt Chart view.

2 Select the task.

3 Click on this task's Task Information icon.

4 Click on the Predecessors tab.

5 Choose Lag/lead type.

6 Enter the value (negative for lead times).

7 Click OK.

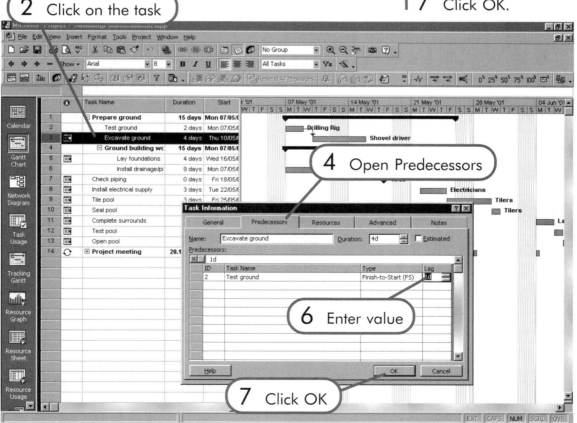

2 Click on the task

4 Open Predecessors

6 Enter value

7 Click OK

Basic steps

1 From the View bar, choose Gantt Chart view.

2 Double-click on a task link to open its Task Dependency dialog box.

3 Enter the lag/lead time required.

4 Click OK.

Quick method of entering Lag/lead times

Lag and lead times can be quickly entered by double-clicking on the link line between two tasks and entering the lag/lead time in the Task Dependency dialog box that is displayed.

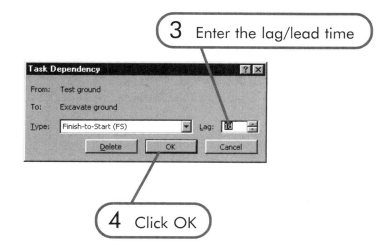

3 Enter the lag/lead time

4 Click OK

Take note

Lag and lead times can have the same relationships as expressed in links, i.e. finish to start (FS), start to start (SS), start to finish (SF) and finish to finish (FF).

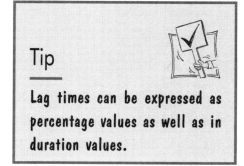

Tip

Lag times can be expressed as percentage values as well as in duration values.

Constraints

A constraint allows you to control the start date or finish date of a particular task. Project 2000 provides a range of constraint types that can be used in your project.

- *As Soon As Possible*   The default constraint type for most projects based on a start date.

- *As Late As Possible*   The default constraint for projects based on a finish date.

- *Finish No Earlier Than* Finish the task either on, or after the date entered.

- *Start No Earlier Than*   Start the task either on or after the date entered.

- *Finish No Later Than*   Finish the task before or on the date entered.

- *Start No Later Than*   Start the task before or no later than the date entered.

- *Must Finish On*   Task must finish on a particular date

- *Must Start On*   Task must start on a particular date.

Take note

Constraints should be used with caution as they can reduce the flexibility of a project and make levelling of over-allocations difficult.

Take note

By default, Project 2000 sets dependent tasks to be completed as soon as possible if the project is scheduled from the start date and as late as possible if the project is scheduled from a finish date.

Basic steps

1 From the View bar, select the Gantt Chart view

2 Click on a task.

3 Click on the task's Task Information icon.

4 Select the Advanced tab.

5 Select the constraint type from the drop down list.

6 Enter the constraint date.

7 Click OK.

Adding constraints to tasks

Use the Task Information dialog box to record constraints against tasks.

> 3 Open the Task Information dialog box

> 4 Go to the Advanced tab

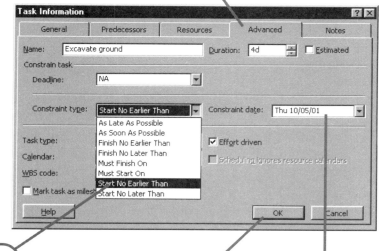

> 5 Select the contraint type

> 7 Click OK

> 6 Enter the date

Take note

The Task Information icon for a task with a constraint is displayed with a red dot in it indicating that a constraint exists. Hover your mouse over this icon to see details of the constraint.

Summary

❑ Linking tasks allows relationships to be clearly expressed.

❑ Dependency links allow you to place rules on the start and finish times of tasks.

❑ Lag times and lead times allow you to plan for time period breaks between dependent tasks.

❑ Constraints allow you to control the start and finish dates of a particular task.

7 Project costs

Resource rates 66

Wage rate rises 71

Project baseline 72

Checking costs 73

Summary 76

Resource rates

Setting the cost of a work resource allows you to enter the standard hourly rate of the resource and the standard hourly overtime rates.

Basic steps

1 Go to the Resource Sheet view.

2 Select the resource.

3 Enter the Std. Rate hourly value.

4 Enter the Ovt. Rate hourly value.

❑ Pay rates should be in the standard currency format e.g. £6.69.

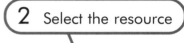

2 Select the resource

3 Enter the Standard Rate

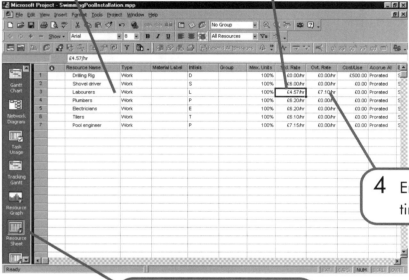

4 Enter the Over-time Rate

1 Click Resource Sheet

Take note

Each task in a project has costs, arising from the resources it uses. Whether they are work (e.g. a person or a piece of machinery) or material resources (e.g. slabs, cement, paint) there will be a cost to them. Costs are important to the success of a project in terms of budget or in determining whether you can use more of or need to reduce the usage of a particular resource.

Project 2000 makes it very straightforward to add a cost to a resource allowing you to manage and review the cost of your project at any time.

Basic steps

1 Go to the Resource Sheet view.

2 From the View menu, select Table: Entry, then Entry.

3 On the Resource sheet, select the re-source to be amended.

4 From the Standard toolbar, click on the Resource Information icon.

5 Click on the Costs tab.

6 Note that the first tab (A) is highlighted in the Cost rate tables – this is the default.

7 Click on tab B.

8 Enter new rates in the Standard Rate and Overtime Rate fields.

9 Click OK.

Setting multiple monetary rates to a resource

A work resource may have different costs depending on the task or project being undertaken. Project 2000 allows you to set up multiple rates for each resource allowing you to choose the set of rates required for a particular task or project.

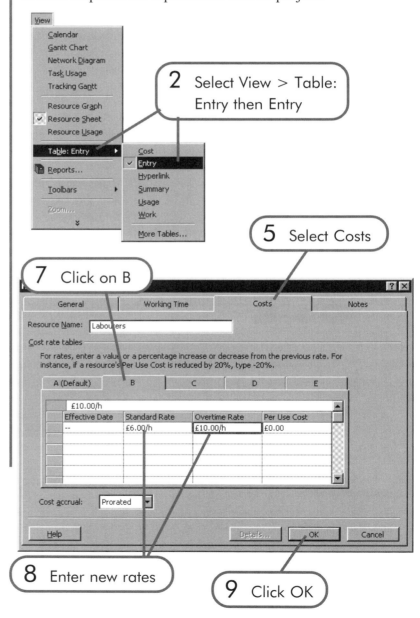

Using a different resource rate

Now that you have successfully entered different rates for a particular resource, you can apply these rates to particular project tasks.

If resources are not shown below tasks, click on the '+' sign in the Task Name field.

Tip

Right-click anywhere in a resource to open its Resource Information dialog box.

Basic steps

1 Open the Task Usage view.

2 Click on the resource name for a task.

3 Click on the Assignment Information icon.

4 Open the General tab.

5 Select the Cost rate table to apply.

6 Click OK.

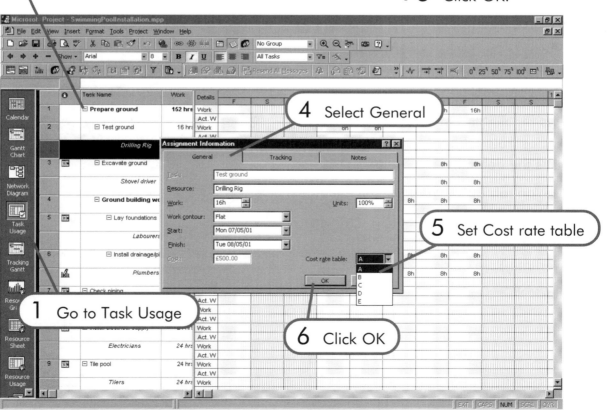

Basic steps

1 From the View bar, choose the Task Usage view.

2 Position the cursor in the column to the right of where the new column is to be placed.

3 From the Insert menu, select Column.

4 From the Column Definition dialog box, select Cost Rate Table.

5 Enter a suitable heading for the column.

6 Choose an alignment for the title and data held in the column.

7 Click OK.

Displaying the cost used for a resource

You may like to display resource rates in the Task Usage and other views. This is especially useful if a resource has different rates applied to different tasks in the project. They can appear anywhere within the table, in a separate column.

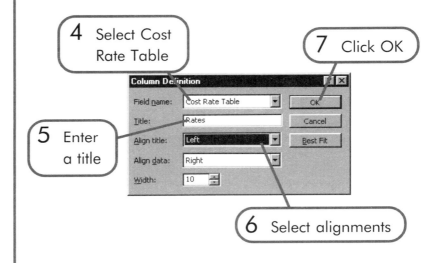

4 Select Cost Rate Table

5 Enter a title

7 Click OK

6 Select alignments

Take note

The above method can be used to display other information fields that you want to include in table views.

Tip

You can now change the rate being used by a resource by simply clicking in the added column and selecting the rate table to be used for the task.

Adding a fixed rate resource

Project 2000 allows you to apply a fixed rate, or 'per-use' cost to a particular resource. An example might be skip hire which is not dependent on an hourly rate but rather on the number of times used in the project.

- A resource can have both hourly rates and per-use costs associated with it.

- Per-use costs can only be associated with work resources (equipment or people).

1   From the View bar, select the Resource Sheet.

2   Click on the resource to have a per-use cost attached.

3   Enter the value to be charged each time the resource is used in the Cost/Use field.

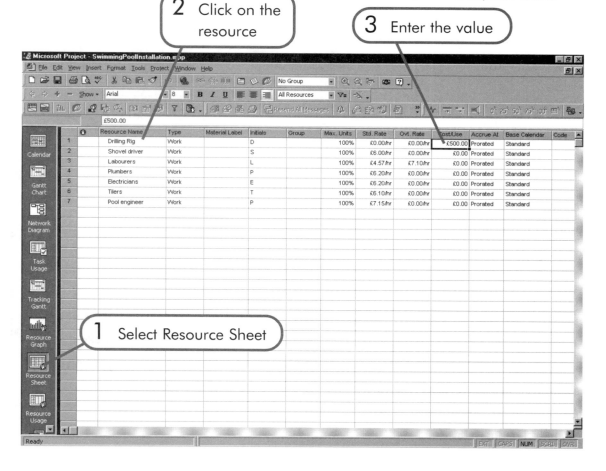

2 Click on the resource

3 Enter the value

1 Select Resource Sheet

Basic steps

1 Go to the Resource Sheet view.

2 Choose the resource.

3 Click on the Resource Information icon.

4 In the Resource Information dialog box, click on the Costs tab.

5 On the next available row, enter a start date for the new rates.

6 Enter the new rates (these will be applied on the date shown).

7 Click OK.

During the lifetime of a long project, project staff might be awarded wage increases, which must be taken in to account in costing. Project 2000 lets you plan timed wage increases into your resource rates.

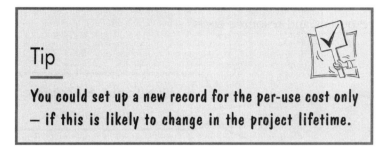

Tip

You could set up a new record for the per-use cost only – if this is likely to change in the project lifetime.

Take note

You can change the value of rates in any of the tabs.

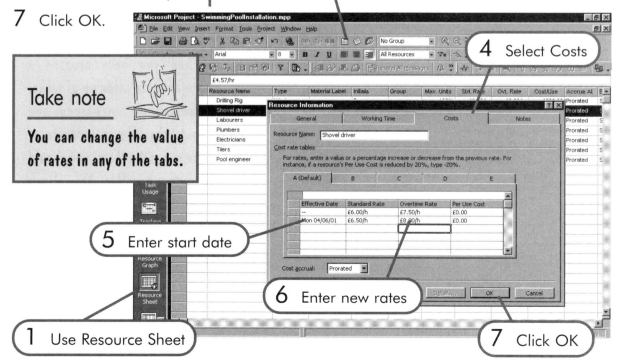

3 Click Resource Information

4 Select Costs

5 Enter start date

6 Enter new rates

7 Click OK

1 Use Resource Sheet

Project baseline

When resources have been set up with rates and fixed costs it is essential to monitor them to ensure that your project is performing to the set budget. Project 2000 allows you to easily manage costs against your project baseline. A baseline for a project shows the original estimates for the project in terms of tasks, resources and resource costs.

Basic steps

1 From the Tools menu, select Tracking, then Save Baseline...

2 Choose the Save baseline radio button.

3 Click OK.

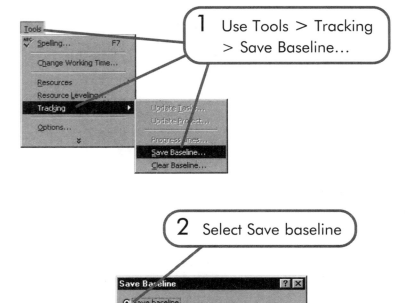

1 Use Tools > Tracking > Save Baseline...

2 Select Save baseline

3 Click OK

Take note

When you have created a project plan made up of tasks, timescales, resources and costs that are as accurate as you can make them, you should create a baseline. This allows you to then track actual costs against these original esti-mates.

Basic steps

1 From the Project menu, click Project Information.

2 Click Statistics…

3 Look at the costing information displayed and compare against baseline and actual values incurred.

4 Click Close.

Checking costs

It is good practice during the lifetime of your project to check costs regularly. This will allow you to make decisions quickly and proactively if a project is slipping or if costs are escalating out of control.

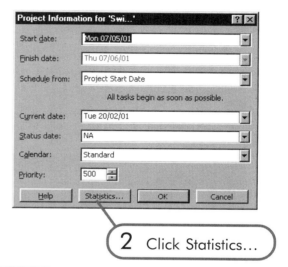

2 Click Statistics…

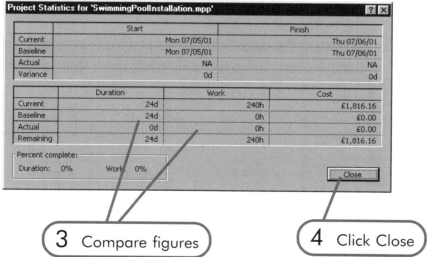

3 Compare figures

4 Click Close

Using Project 2000 reports to view costs

Basic steps

Project 2000 comes with a powerful suite of project reports that can easily be used to provide valuable project information.

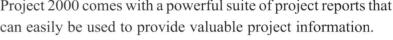

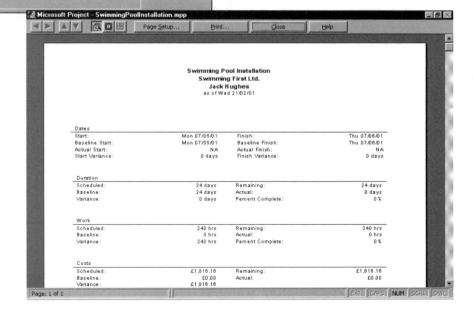

1 From the View menu, choose Reports.

2 Click the Overview... icon.

3 Click Select.

4 Click the Project Summary icon.

5 Click Select.

6 View a great project summary report.

7 Click Close.

8 Click Close (again!).

Basic steps

1 From the View menu, choose Reports.

2 Click on a report type.

3 Click Select.

4 Select a report.

5 Click Select.

6 Click Page Setup.

7 Click on the Header tab.

8 Make changes as appropriate.

9 Repeat steps 7-8 for the Footer tab.

10 Click OK.

Headers and footers

Headers and footers can be added to Project 2000 reports. Similar to use with views, this enhances and customises reports allowing you to make Project 2000 organisation specific.

6 Go to Page Setup

7 Switch to the Header tab

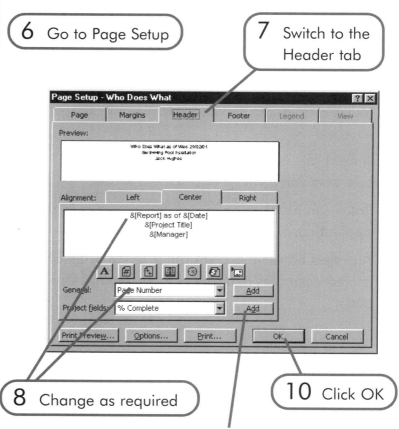

8 Change as required

10 Click OK

Click to add fields to the report

Tip

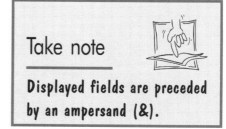

The Page Setup dialog box also allows you to add special fields such as a page number and a total page count. Spend time experimenting with these.

Take note

Displayed fields are preceded by an ampersand (&).

Summary

❑ Project resources have costs associated with them.

❑ A work resource can be a person or a piece of machinery whose use is measured in terms of time.

❑ A material resource can be items whose use is measured in terms of quantity, weight, etc.

❑ Work resources can have both standard and over-time rates associated with them.

❑ Multiple rates can be associated with work resources.

❑ A fixed rate can be applied to a resource that has a cost associated with it each time it is used.

❑ Rates can be timed, allowing for increases to be applied easily.

❑ A project baseline is a snapshot of the original project estimates in terms of tasks, resources and costs.

8 Formatting projects

Changing task names 78

Working with fields 80

Formatting text 84

Formatting Gantt Charts 85

Sorting project tasks 87

Summary 88

Changing task names

Once you've created your project, identified your tasks and their durations and assigned resources, and saved a baseline, the project is ready to be implemented. It might be the case that, as you begin, names used for tasks need changing to something more meaningful to the task being undertaken. Similarly, resource names may change, especially if you're using the names of individuals who may have left your organisation or been transferred to another project.

Basic steps

1 From the View bar, click on the Gantt Chart view.

2 Click on the Task Name field to be changed.

3 Press [F2].

4 Press [Backspace] to delete the old name.

5 Type the new name and press [Enter].

5 Enter the new name

2 Click on task to be changed

1 Select Gantt Chart

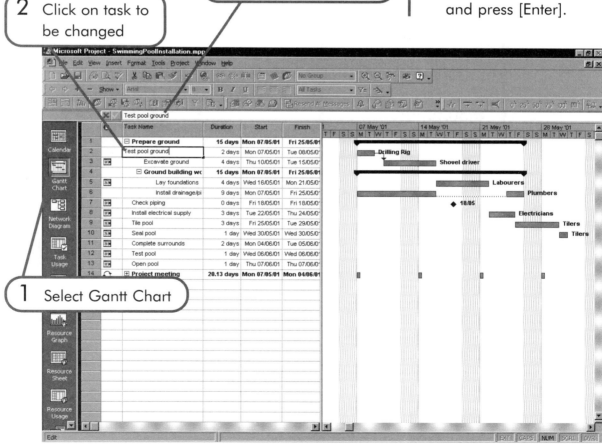

Basic steps

Changing resource names

1 From the View bar, click on the Resource Sheet view.

2 From the View menu, select Table: Entry then Entry.

3 Select the resource and press [F2].

4 Amend the Resource Name as appropriate.

5 Press [Enter].

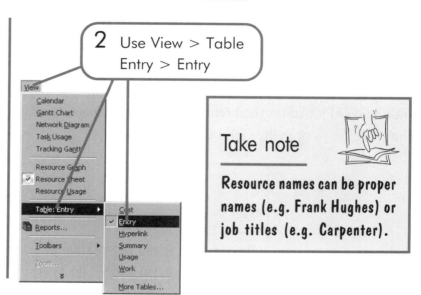

2 Use View > Table Entry > Entry

Take note

Resource names can be proper names (e.g. Frank Hughes) or job titles (e.g. Carpenter).

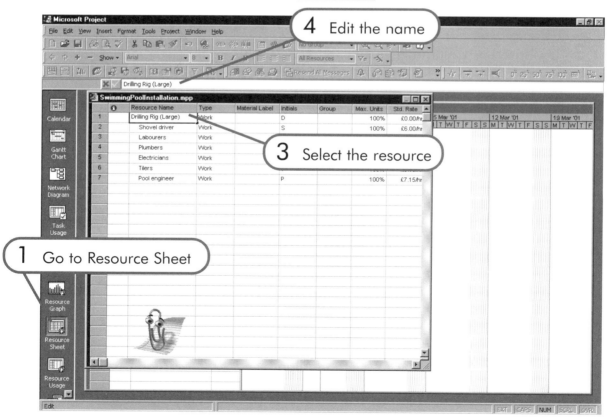

4 Edit the name

3 Select the resource

1 Go to Resource Sheet

Working with fields

Project 2000 provides a wide range of views that are likely to cover most of your needs in terms of providing information to project stakeholders. However, there will be times when you will wish to amend a view to show extra information or perhaps hide some of it. Adding and removing field columns in any of the sheet views or in the Gantt Chart view is easy.

Basic steps

- ❑ To add a column
- 1 Select the Gantt Chart or any sheet view.
- 2 Click on the column to the right of where you want to add one.
- 3 From the Insert menu, choose Column…
- 4 In the Column Definition dialog box use the drop-down list to select a new field.
- 5 Give the field a title.
- 6 Set the alignments.
- 7 Click OK.

Tip

Double-click in the right border of a field title to set the field size to fit the largest item held in it.

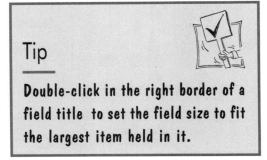

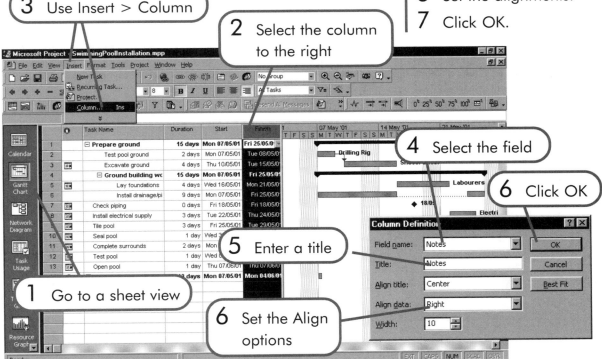

80

Basic steps

❑ To hide a column

1 From the View bar, select the Gantt Chart view (or any sheet view).

2 Select the column to be hidden (click on its name).

3 From the Edit menu, choose Hide Column.

Take note

When you hide a column in a view, the field data still exists and can be added back at any stage. No data is actually deleted.

③ Use Edit > Hide Column

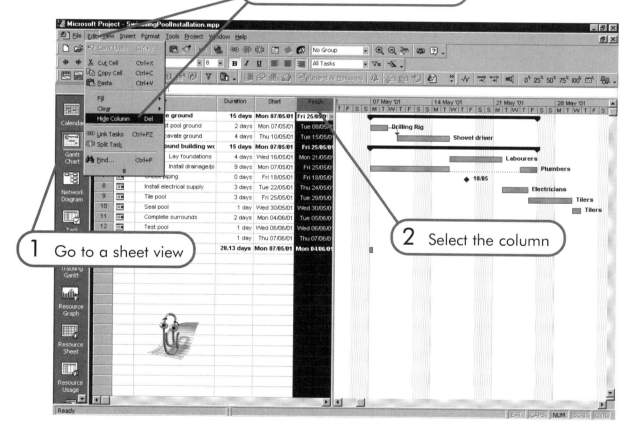

① Go to a sheet view

② Select the column

Changing field name and alignment details

Project 2000 allows you to amend an existing view by changing the name, alignment and width options of fields. This way you can use terminology that is specific to your particular organisation or industry rather than simply accepting the defaults provided by Project 2000.

1 Choose the Gantt Chart view.

2 Double-click the field heading to be changed.

3 In the Column Definition dialog box make any changes.

4 Click OK.

1 Select Gantt Chart

2 Double-click on the heading

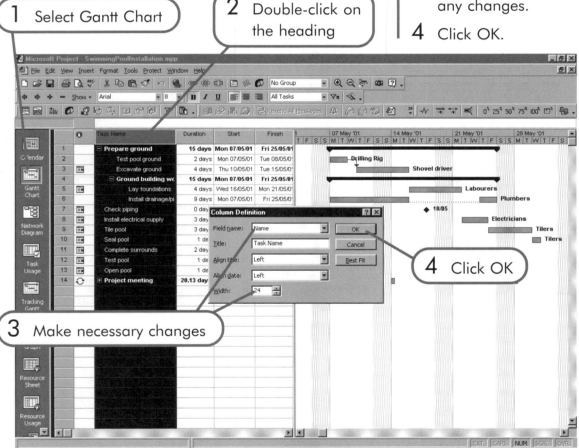

3 Make necessary changes

4 Click OK

Basic steps

1 Select More Views… then Task Sheet view.

2 From the View menu, select Table Entry then More Tables.

3 Select Summary.

4 Click on Copy…

5 Enter the name as *'New Summary'*.

6 Select the Cost and Work fields and click Delete Row to delete them.

7 Click on the next available field and from the drop-down list, choose Notes.

8 Click OK then Apply.

❑ The Task Sheet view now uses this table.

Tip

To return a view to using its original table, select the table as above and click Apply.

Modifying tables used in views

Project 2000 comes with a number of tables, reflecting both tasks and resources, that are automatically used in the various views. However you might wish to modify an existing table or create a new one to bring together useful fields from different tables within Project 2000.

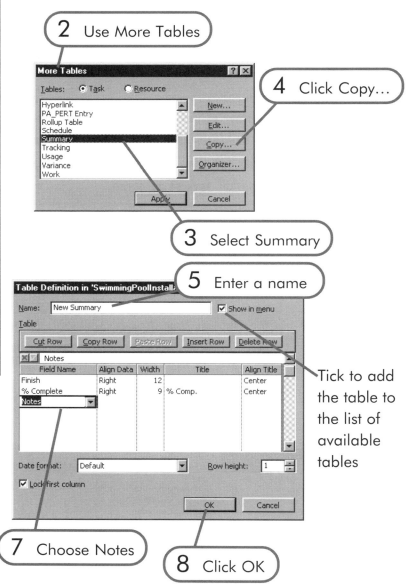

2 Use More Tables

4 Click Copy…

3 Select Summary

5 Enter a name

Tick to add the table to the list of available tables

7 Choose Notes

8 Click OK

Formatting text

Project 2000 automatically provides formatting for all views. Should you wish to change the format of a view, say to increase the text font size, you can easily carry this out.

From the Format menu you can change chart colours, and text styles for particular categories by accessing the Text Styles and Detail Styles menu options.

Tip

To change the format of one task or resource, simply highlight the row and format as above. You can then use the Format Painter (on the Standard toolbar) to copy this format to another task or resource.

Basic steps

1 From the View bar, choose a view.

2 Highlight the table information to be formatted by clicking on the top left cell to be included, pressing [Shift] and clicking on the bottom right cell to be included.

3 From the Format menu choose Font.

4 Change the Font, Font Style and Size to suit.

5 Click OK.

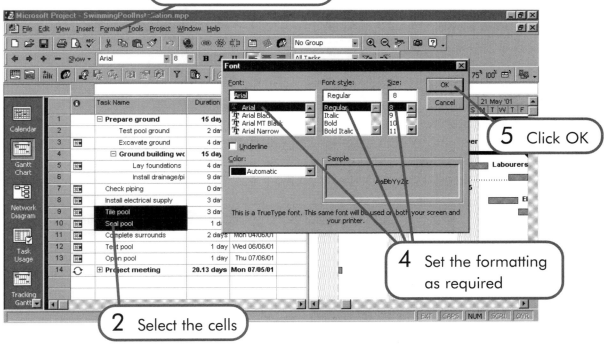

3 Use Format > Font

5 Click OK

4 Set the formatting as required

2 Select the cells

Formatting Gantt Charts

1 From the View bar, select the Gantt Chart view.

2 From the Format menu, choose Bar Styles.

3 Click on the Appearance column for the Task field.

4 Change the Start, Middle and End of the bar to suit your needs – try changing the pattern used for the bar.

5 Change the colours as appropriate.

6 Carry out steps 3 to 5 to format other bar styles.

7 Click OK.

The Gantt Chart is one of the most useful and widely used views in Project 2000. Formatting of it is straightforward and easy.

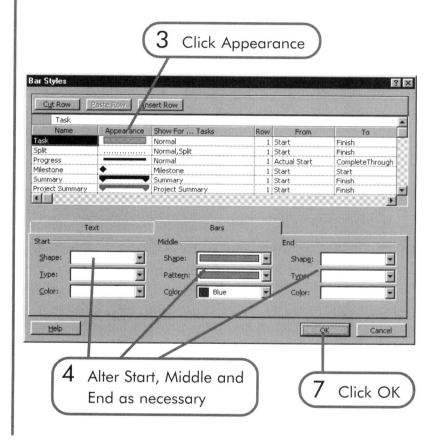

3 Click Appearance

4 Alter Start, Middle and End as necessary

7 Click OK

Tip

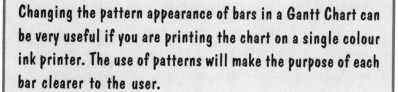

Changing the pattern appearance of bars in a Gantt Chart can be very useful if you are printing the chart on a single colour ink printer. The use of patterns will make the purpose of each bar clearer to the user.

Using the GanttChart Wizard

You can also carry out some formatting using the GanttChart Wizard.

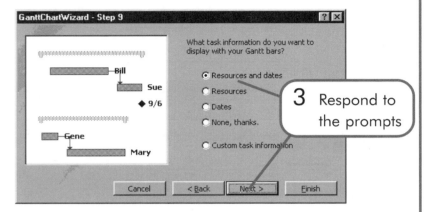

Changing the appearance of linked tasks

You can easily change the way that linked tasks appear on a Gantt Chart. This has the effect of highlighting the links, making them easier to follow.

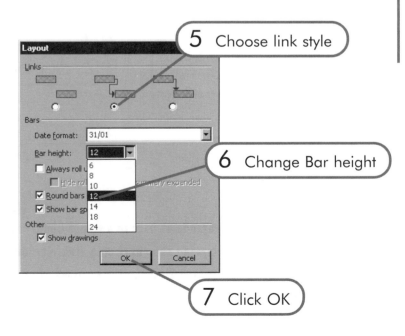

Basic steps

- ❑ Using the Wizard
1 Choose the Gantt Chart view.
2 Click the GanttChart Wizard button on the Formatting toolbar.
3 Follow the instructions presented on screen.
- ❑ Formatting linked tasks
4 From the Format menu, choose Layout.
5 Choose your preferred style for arrows linking tasks.
6 Change the height of the bars.
7 Click OK.

Sorting project tasks

1 From the View bar
   choose More Views...
   then Task Sheet view.

2 From the Project menu
   choose Sort then Sort
   By...

3 In the Sort by field,
   select Start.

4 In the Then by field
   select Resource
   Names.

5 Click Sort.

❑ Note the tasks sorted
   by start date and then
   by resource within
   start date.

Once you've entered all your project tasks and assigned resource you're likely to want to customise some of the available views to order your tasks in different ways. This might mean printing tasks in start date order, by resource or by some other order.

2 Use Project > Sort
   > Sort By...

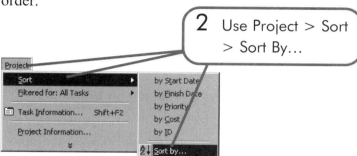

3 Select Start

5 Click Sort

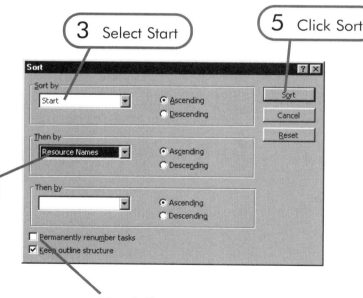

4 Select Resource
   Names

Check if you want your project
tasks renumbered after sorting –
this isn't particularly necessary

Take note

Sorting tasks in one view will have no effect when viewing them in a different view within the same project.

Summary

❑ Task and resource names can be amended during the lifetime of the project.

❑ Fields can be added to a view, and their names or alignment can be changed.

❑ Fields in a view can be hidden.

❑ All views allow for quick formatting of font, text colour and size as well as other formatting options.

❑ Views use tables and these tables can be modified or used to create new tables.

❑ The appearance of links in a Gantt Chart can be changed.

❑ Use the Wizard to format your Gantt Chart.

❑ Use Bar Styles on the Format menu to change the look of the bars in your Gantt Chart.

❑ Sorting project tasks allows you to display a view in a more suitable format to suit your project needs.

9 Project charts

Producing project charts 90

The Gantt Chart view 91

Calendar view 92

Network Diagram 93

Resource Sheet view 94

Resource Graph view 95

Resource Name Form 96

The Task Usage view 97

Task Details form 98

Tracking Gantt view 99

Resource Usage view 100

Filtering information 101

Summary 104

Producing project charts

Earlier chapters dealt with Project 2000's three main view types: task, resource, and assignment views. It allows you to print reports, charts and graphs to represent all project information in a number of ways. The difficulty is often deciding which format is best suited to the task.

In general, charts and graphs are visual and provide an easy way to get a summarised view of your project. This type of reporting mechanism might prove useful to senior managers who only need a very generic view of your project. It might also be useful to pin graphic information on walls in site offices and project offices as they offer a visual representation of the status of the project and its tasks.

Table and form views are more suited to the provision of in-depth detailed reports with analysis fields. This type of reporting mechanism will be used by those responsible for the management and monitoring of the project on a daily basis.

Tip

Generally, you'll use a standard group of charts and reports which you have found particularly useful when managing projects. If these are used uniformly, and often, then you will probably have found as good a way as any of reporting on your project.

Take note

There's no hard and fast rule on the type of information provided for project stakeholders. Only through practice and knowledge of individuals and their requirements will you make the right reporting decisions.

The Gantt Chart view

The Gantt Chart view is a combination view showing task information in table layout form as well as showing graphical tasks over time. It is a great starting view and is a good place to create your initial project plan.

The Gantt Chart view is the common view used to add and edit tasks, assign resources and link project tasks. It is also used to actually see the progress of tasks visually.

Summary task

Task durations

Task resources

Timescales

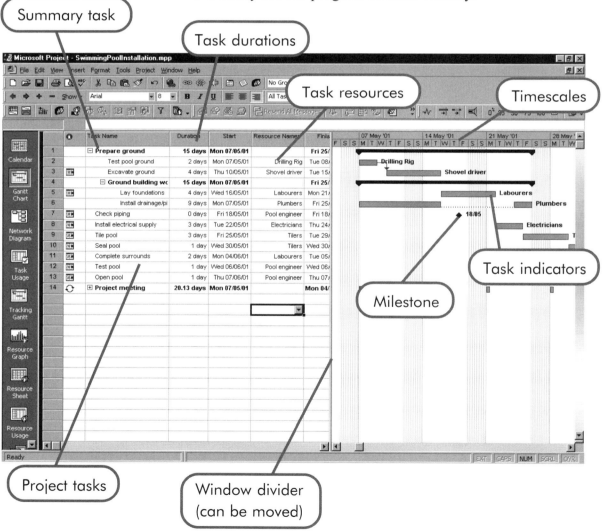

Task indicators

Milestone

Project tasks

Window divider
(can be moved)

Calendar view

This view shows project tasks in a typical calendar layout, month by month over the lifetime of the project. Four weeks of tasks are shown on each screen.

The calendar view is useful should you be looking to determine a work plan for a single week or over a number of weeks.

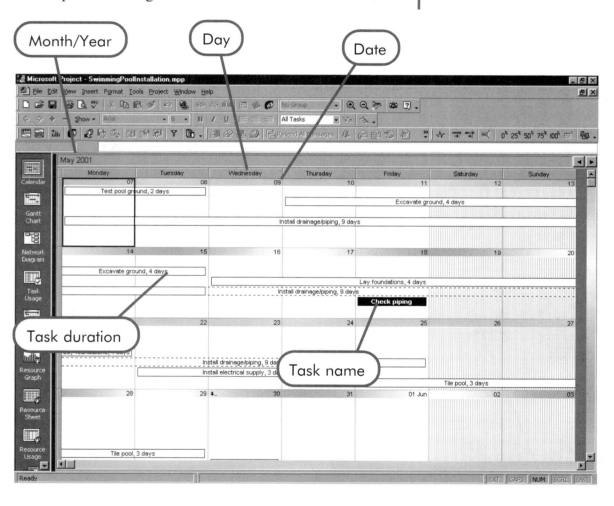

Network Diagram

This view shows all tasks, each in a separate box with details of start and finish dates, resources used and expected duration. Any task dependencies are also shown.

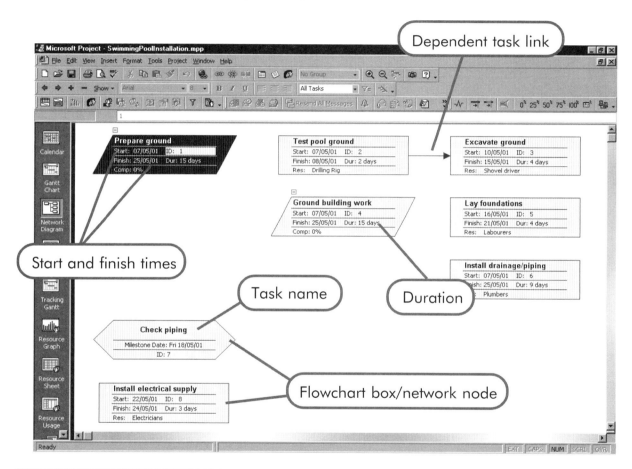

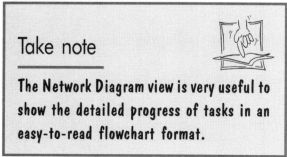

Take note

The Network Diagram view is very useful to show the detailed progress of tasks in an easy-to-read flowchart format.

Resource Sheet view

The Resource Sheet view is used to allow you to see a complete schedule of project resources and their associated costs.

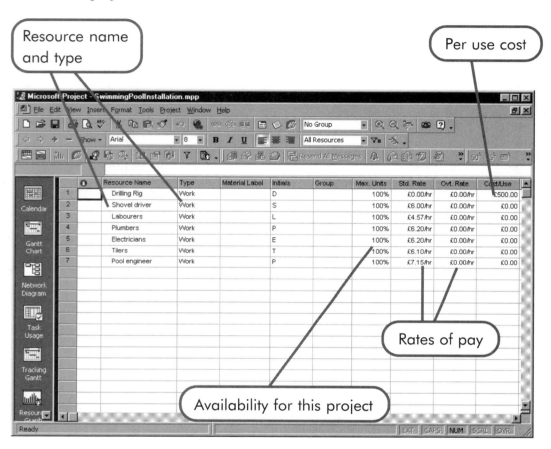

Resource name and type

Per use cost

Rates of pay

Availability for this project

Resource Graph view

The Resource Graph view allows you to determine the work allocation of a resource or group of resources over time.

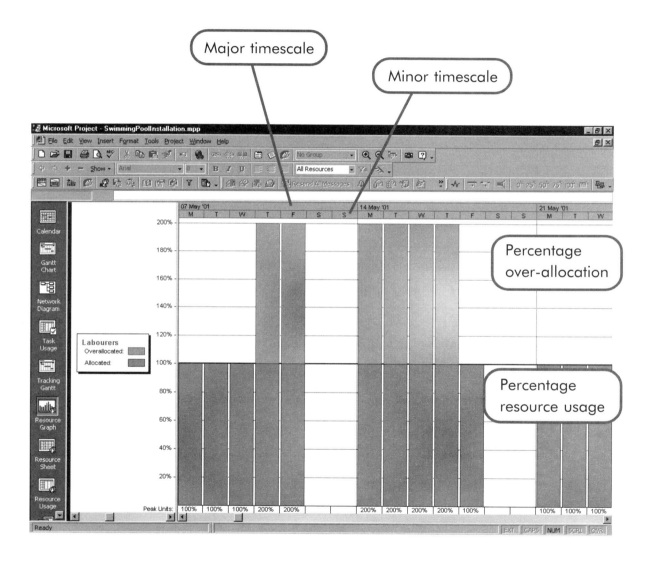

Resource Name Form

The Resource Name Form view allows you to change the name
of a resource and have this name change reflected throughout
every project task using the resource. The Resource Name Form
gives a quick way of determining the tasks that each resource
will be working on in the project lifetime.

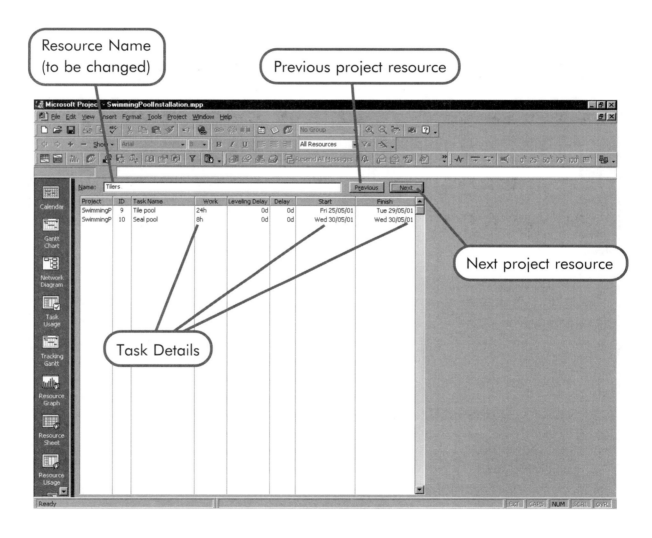

The Task Usage view

This view provides a great way to monitor each task and the project resources assigned to it. This view is great for determining the tasks required to be completed by each resource. Use the Sort option in the Project menu to sort tasks by resources.

Each task with a start date, finish date and duration

Start and finish date for resource

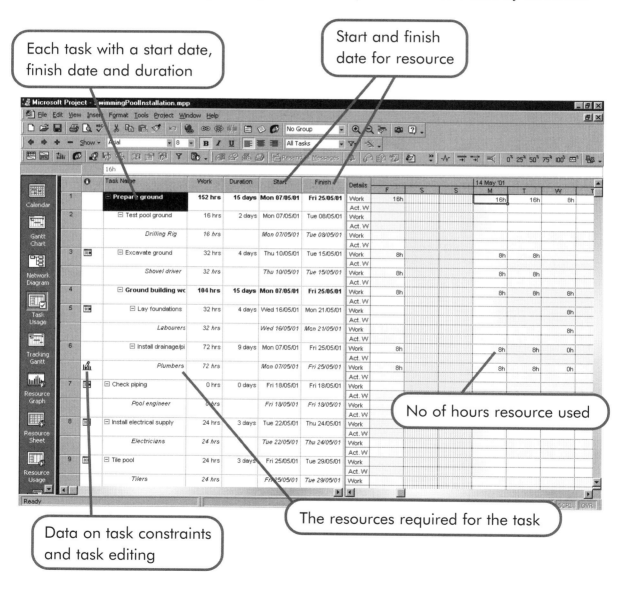

No of hours resource used

Data on task constraints and task editing

The resources required for the task

Task Details form

For each task, the Task Details Form view gives detailed information about the task, its predecessors and successors and the resources that it uses. You can use this view to edit task details. By splitting the Project 2000 window, you can use this option to display detailed task information at the bottom of another view.

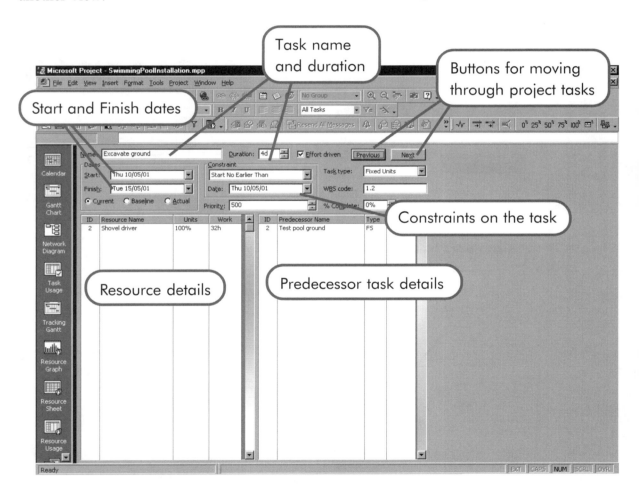

Tracking Gantt view

This view is particularly useful for visually measuring planned versus actual start dates and durations for tasks. Each bar is shown in two colours rather than one, placed one on top of the other. The first bar shows the actual start date and duration of the task while the second bar shows the baseline detail for the task. The Tracking Gantt Chart view is excellent for managing project slippage.

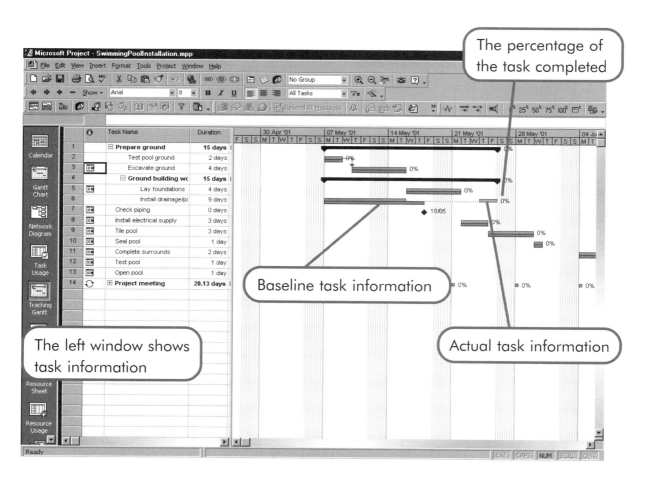

The percentage of the task completed

Baseline task information

Actual task information

The left window shows task information

Resource Usage view

Controlling the usage of resources in a project is critical. This view allows you to easily view resources, their associated costs and any over-allocations. This way you can plan ahead perhaps by levelling your project resources. This view is useful to help you determine any free time that a resource might have which could be used in other projects.

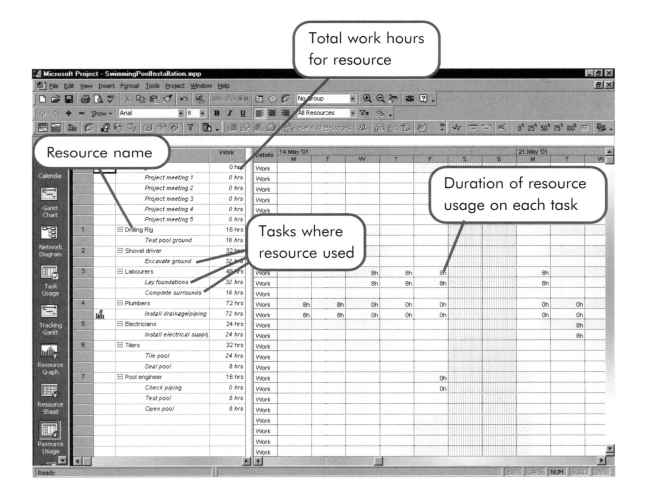

Total work hours for resource

Resource name

Duration of resource usage on each task

Tasks where resource used

Filtering information

Select the Gantt Chart view.

2 From the Project menu, select Filtered for: All Tasks.

3 Choose a filter criterion from the list.

Or

4 Click on the More Filters option to see a full range of filters.

5 There are two sets of filters – select Task or Resource.

6 Choose an appropriate filter and click on Apply.

❑ To remove the filter on your view, change the criterion to All Tasks.

Applying a filter is a good way to focus on specific project tasks or resources. Filters do not delete any project information. They simply act as a mask for information. Project 2000 allows you to filter project data in many formats. This example shows filters being used in the Gantt Chart view.

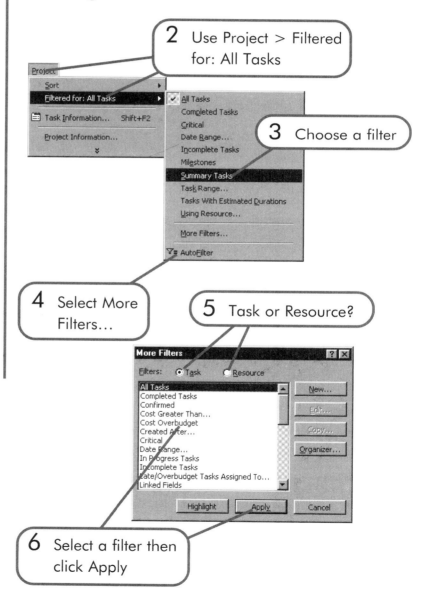

2 Use Project > Filtered for: All Tasks

3 Choose a filter

4 Select More Filters...

5 Task or Resource?

6 Select a filter then click Apply

Applying an interactive filter

An interactive filter allows you to specify a criterion, and, each time the filter is run, the user will be asked to enter a value into a dialog box. This value then becomes the condition for the filter to be applied.

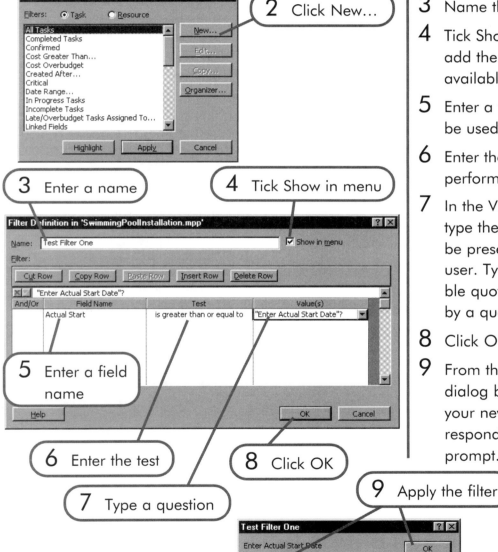

1 Open the More Filters dialog box as shown opposite.

2 Click on New…

3 Name the new filter.

4 Tick Show in menu to add the filter to the available filters list.

5 Enter a field name to be used in the filter.

6 Enter the test to be performed.

7 In the Values field, type the question to be presented to the user. Type it in double quotes, followed by a question mark.

8 Click OK.

9 From the More Filters dialog box, apply your new filter and respond to the filter's prompt.

Basic steps

1 From the Formatting toolbar, click AutoFilter.

2 Click the arrow by a field heading to open its drop-down list.

3 Select a value.

4 Watch your information being filtered automatically.

Applying an AutoFilter

If you want to use the flexibility of filters within your project without necessarily creating filters yourself, Project 2000 provides a great tool that makes filtering project information easy. AutoFilters allow you to filter a subset of data dependent on field values.

> ## Take note
>
> AutoFilters do not work in Resource Graph, Network Diagrams, or any of the form views.

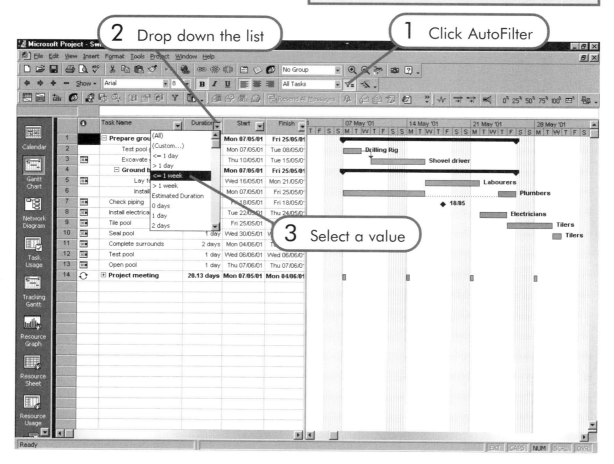

2 Drop down the list

1 Click AutoFilter

3 Select a value

Summary

❑ Project 2000 has a comprehensive suite of views designed to satisfy most project reporting needs.

❑ Task views can enable you to effectively manage the time taken to complete project tasks.

❑ Resource views allow you to effectively manage project resources in terms of the resources allocated to each task.

❑ The Resource Name form allows you to quickly change the name of a resource throughout the project data.

❑ Filtering information allows you to focus on specific project tasks or resources.

10 Keeping on track

Project baselines 106

Project information 107

Saving an interim plan 109

Monitoring project tasks 110

Monitoring project costs 113

Summary 114

Project baselines

It is essential, if you are planning to monitor progress using Project 2000, that you create a baseline for your project. A baseline is a 'line in the sand' from which you can measure your project's progress in terms of tasks completed, as well as the usage and cost of resources. Baseline information, when matched against work in progress, gives you a great tool for ensuring that your project is completed within set budgets. If you've not already saved a baseline with your project, do it now.

Baseline information saved includes task start and finish dates, durations, costs, split tasks, work, timephased work and timephased costs (Timephased costs/resources occur on tasks over a particular time period). Resource information saved includes work, costs, timephased work and timephased costs.

Basic steps

1 From the Tools menu, choose Tracking.

2 Click on Save Baseline...

3 Select Entire project.

4 Click OK.

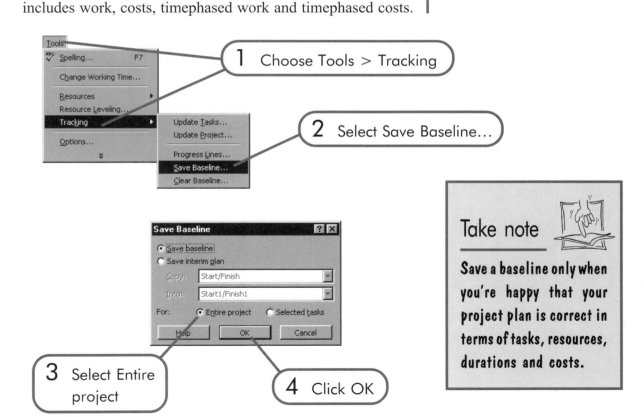

1 Choose Tools > Tracking

2 Select Save Baseline...

3 Select Entire project

4 Click OK

Take note

Save a baseline only when you're happy that your project plan is correct in terms of tasks, resources, durations and costs.

Project information

1 Select the Gantt Chart view.

2 From the View menu, select Toolbars then Tracking menu.

3 Select a task on which progress is to be tracked.

4 Click the 25%, 50%, 75%, or 100% button to indicate how much of the task has been completed.

The Tracking Gantt view allows you to quickly track progress. To enter the actual progress of tasks in your project is very easy using the basic Gantt Chart view as the toolbar provides a number of icons that record task tracking.

● To update task completion in increments of 1%, select the task, right-click on it and choose the **Task Information** menu. In the **General** tab, update the percentage complete value as appropriate.

Click Project Statistics for a snapshot of statistics for the project at the selected time

4 Click a percent button

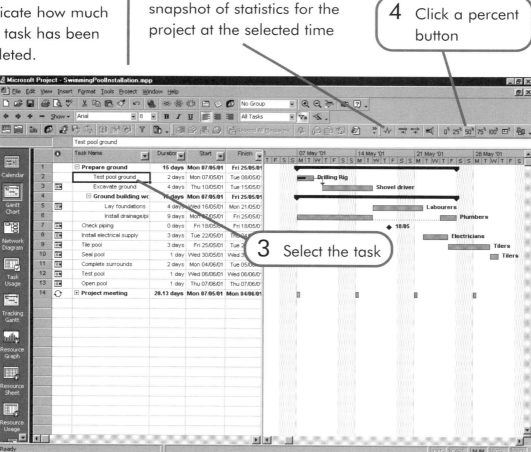

3 Select the task

Using the Update Tasks button

The Tracking toolbar allows you to easily update a task's start date, finish date and duration. Both the Gantt Chart and Tracking Gantt Chart reflect the changes made. When you alter the start date, finish date or duration of a task the following changes are automatically made:

- If the actual duration is less than the planned duration then the duration remaining will be *planned* minus *actual*.

- If you enter an actual finish date, Project 2000 assumes the task is complete and changes the scheduled finish date to the date entered – the task then shows 100% complete.

- If you enter an actual start date for a task, the planned start date is moved to equal this date.

- If the actual duration equals the scheduled duration then the task is considered complete and is marked as 100%.

Basic steps

1 Select a task to amend.

2 Click on the Update Tasks button.

3 Update the Actual Start: and Finish dates as appropriate.

4 Click OK.

> **Take note**
>
> **Completed tasks have the Indicators fields ticked.**

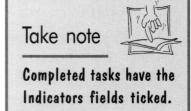

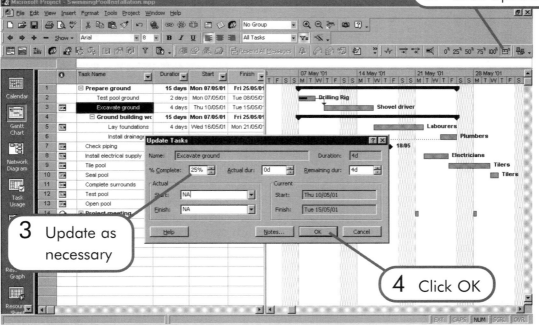

108

Basic steps

1 From the Tools menu, select Tracking then Save Baseline…

2 Click on the Save interim plan radio button.

3 Click on the Entire project radio button.

4 Choose the plan dates to be saved from the drop-down list (For plans 1–10).

5 Click OK.

Saving an interim plan

A baseline plan gives you details of your project when it was originally set up, an interim plan however, provides you with a snapshot of your project at a point further on in its life when actual progress information has been recorded. An interim plan is a snapshot of task start and finish dates. You can compare details on the baseline plan with an interim plan.

Each project can have a maximum of 10 interim plans saved.

Interim plan comparison is useful only for comparing start and finish dates. An interim plan cannot be used to compare costs or work.

Use the Clear Baseline menu option in the Tracking menu to erase the project baseline. You can then save a new baseline as required.

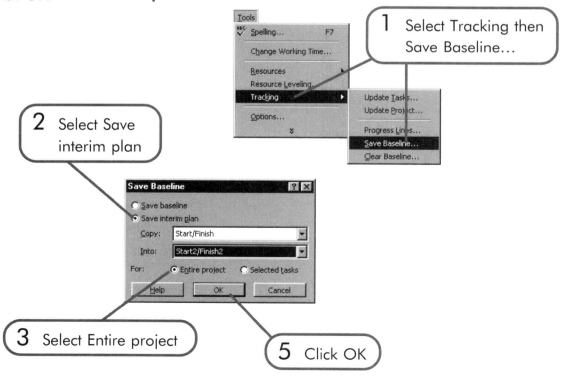

Monitoring project tasks

One of the most fundamental monitoring techniques in project management involves determining any slippage that has occurred in project tasks. This allows you to determine whether the project will still finish on schedule or whether remedial action needs to be taken.

1 From the View bar, select the Tracking Gantt view.

2 Choose a task where the actual start date exceeds the baseline start date.

3 The task progress line is shown in blue.

4 The baseline plan is shown in grey.

❑ Note the variance.

Tip

Use the AutoFilter drop-down box on the toolbar to display in your view only those tasks that are slipping.

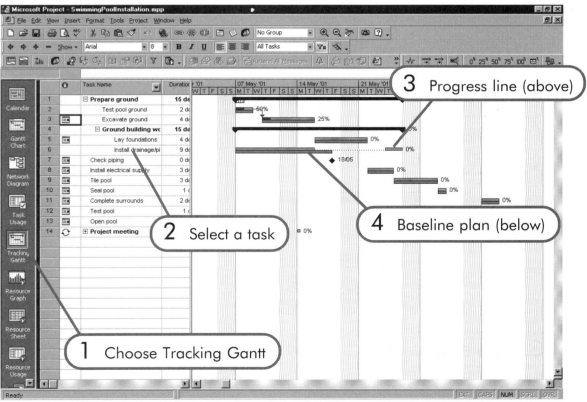

3 Progress line (above)

2 Select a task

4 Baseline plan (below)

1 Choose Tracking Gantt

Basic steps

1 From the View bar, select More Views…

2 Choose Task Sheet.

3 Click Apply.

4 Click on the Start field.

5 From the Insert menu, choose Column.

6 Insert the 'Baseline Start' field.

7 Click OK.

8 Repeat step 4-6 for the 'Baseline Finish' field.

Comparing planned with current progress

Project 2000 allows you to quickly compare your baseline detail with the current status of the project. For this you'll use the Task Sheet view and add the baseline start and finish dates.

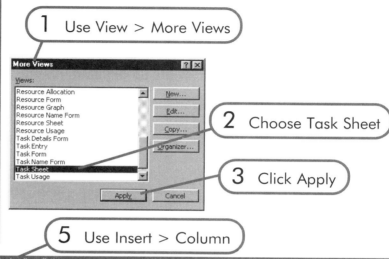

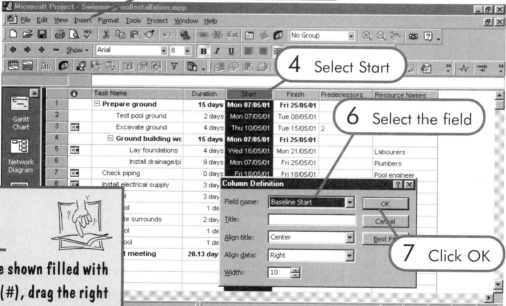

Take note

If columns are shown filled with hash symbols (#), drag the right side of the column header and the data will be displayed.

Interim plan and current progress

Project 2000 allows you to quickly compare one of your saved interim plans with the current status of the project. Again, you'll use the Task Sheet view to complete this comparison – the task start and finish dates compared with the first interim plan's start and finish dates.

Follow the steps on page 111, but this time insert the 'Start1' and 'Finish1' fields. The output should be similar to this.

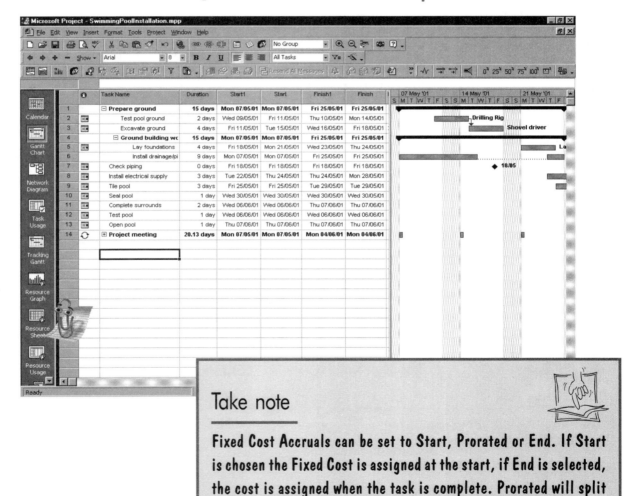

Take note

Fixed Cost Accruals can be set to Start, Prorated or End. If Start is chosen the Fixed Cost is assigned at the start, if End is selected, the cost is assigned when the task is complete. Prorated will split the cost in equal amounts across the time the task takes.

Basic steps

1 From the View menu, choose Table: Cost then Cost.

2 From the View bar, choose More Views… then Task Sheet view

❑ Note the cost variance information shown.

Monitoring project costs

It is essential to the success of your project that costs are kept within budget. In terms of profitability and cash flow management this is extremely important. On some projects you will be paid at certain milestones, therefore cost monitoring becomes even more important. Project 2000 provides all the tools to monitor cost variance effectively.

● Costing information provided by Project 2000 is excellent if you are managing a project on a tight budget. However, if you have a project accountant on board, don't be surprised if the information produced is used only as part of the bigger project cost picture.

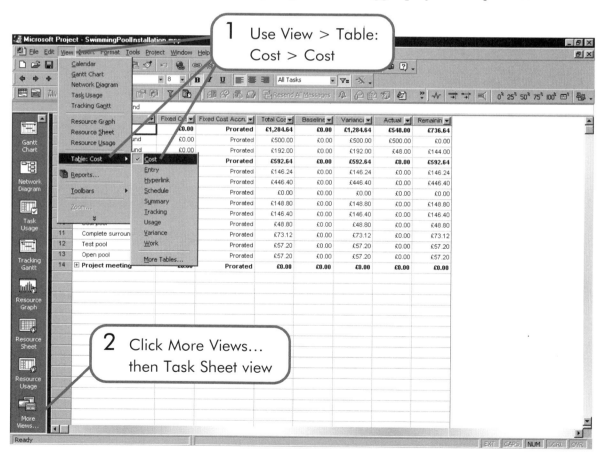

Summary

❑ A baseline allows you to monitor project progress.

❑ The Tracking Gantt view enables you to easily monitor task slippage.

❑ The Tracking toolbar provides useful tools to enable the recording of actual project progress.

❑ An interim plan is snapshot of your project at a particular date in its lifetime.

❑ Project 2000 will enable you to monitor your costs efficiently.

11 Multiple projects

Multiple projects 116

Creating a master project 117

Viewing a master project 119

Deleting sub-projects 121

Summary 124

Multiple projects

Project 2000 is a great tool for managing individual projects. If you decide to use the application to manage all work carried out within your organisation then it becomes more than a single project management tool and enables you to control resources throughout your organisation covering multi-projects.

In Chapter 5 you looked at sharing resources across multiple projects, now you'll consider consolidating projects together into what is known as a 'master project'. A master project is great for letting you view all project tasks in the one place. These will all be part of separate projects (sub-projects) which are being run and managed independently. When these projects are updated the updated information is instantly made available to the master project.

A master project is a great tool to allow senior operational managers a complete overview of the work being carried out within an organisation at any particular point in time.

Take note

Many organisations will choose to manage multiple projects by keeping them completely independent and simply using the printed report and views from each project to manage the overall workload of the organisation. This is fine — it's really up to each individual organisation's preferred method of working.

Basic steps

1. From the File menu, choose New.
2. Select the Blank Project icon.
3. Click OK.
4. In the Project Information dialog box enter an appropriate project start date.
5. Click OK.
6. From the File menu, choose Save As…
7. Name your master project.
8. Click Save.

Creating a master project

Creating a master project is easy using Project 2000 and follows the same rules required to set up any standard project.

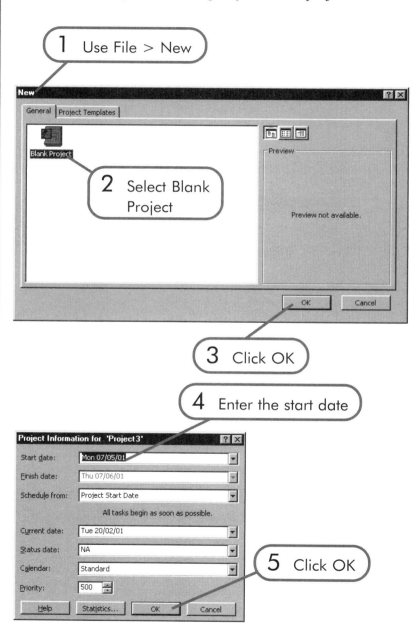

1 Use File > New

2 Select Blank Project

3 Click OK

4 Enter the start date

5 Click OK

Tip

When naming a master project ensure that you give it a name that will easily identify it as being a consolidation of all, or a number, of your current projects.

Inserting a sub-project into a master project

Now that you've successfully created and named your master project you can simply 'slot in' sub-projects to populate this master project with useful project information.

1 From the Insert menu, choose Project…

2 From the Insert Project dialog box, select a project to be inserted.

3 Click Insert.

❑ Your project is now inserted into the master project.

4 Complete steps 2–3 for any further projects to be added.

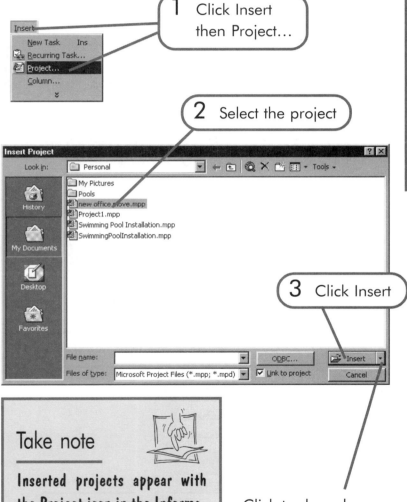

1 Click Insert then Project…

2 Select the project

3 Click Insert

Click to drop down Insert options

Take note

Inserted projects appear with the Project icon in the Information field. Hover over this with your mouse to see the full project filename and path.

Tip

The Insert Project dialog box works like Windows Explorer, allowing you to move around folders, and move up levels. You can also create new folders here.

Basic steps

1 From the View bar, choose the Gantt Chart view.

2 Click on the first task (sub-project).

3 From the Formatting toolbar, click Show All Subtasks.

❏ Your inserted project tasks are now shown.

Viewing a master project

When you first add sub-projects to a master project file and view them in the Gantt Chart view, they are shown as single task line entries with one summary task per project. You can easily view all tasks that make up each inserted project.

> ## Tip
>
> **You can show and hide subtasks by clicking the summary tasks' outline symbol in the Task Name field ('+' or '-').**

3 Use Show > All Subtasks

2 Select the first task

1 Choose Gantt Chart

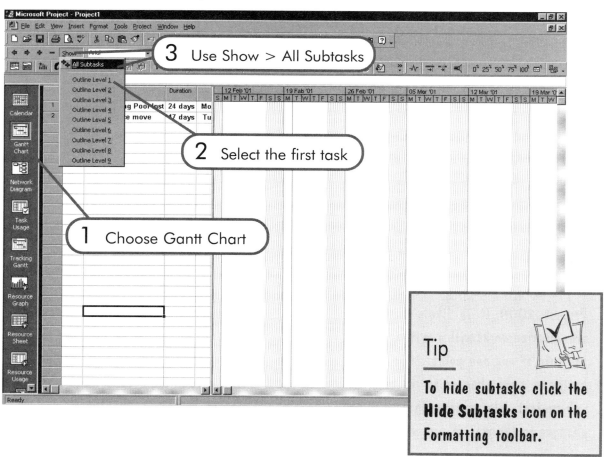

> ## Tip
>
> To hide subtasks click the **Hide Subtasks** icon on the Formatting toolbar.

Viewing more than one project

Once you've created a master project and inserted sub-projects into it, you'll want a quick way to see a complete overview of master project tasks. This will allow you to view the work that will be carried out through the lifetime of all live projects, or in a particular time slice, say a week or a month.

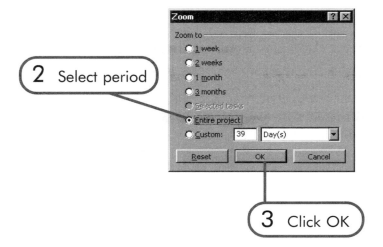

 2 Select period

3 Click OK

1 From the View menu, select Zoom.

2 In the Zoom dialog box, select the period to be shown.

3 Click OK.

❑ Project 2000 adjusts the major and minor scales of your Gantt Chart to show project details as requested by your 'zoom to' criteria.

Tip

If you use the master project option in Project 2000 it is likely that your organisation works with a number of live projects at any one point. It is always better to make changes to the original sub-project files rather than making changes to the master project file.

Tip

To ensure that sub-projects cannot be changed in a master project, insert them as read-only. This option is available in the drop-down list on the Insert button in the Insert Project dialog box (see page 118).

Basic steps

1 From the View bar, click on the Gantt Chart view.

2 Click on the summary task (sub-project) to be removed.

3 Press [Delete].

Or

4 From the Edit menu, choose Delete Task.

Deleting sub-projects

Project 2000 provides an easy method to remove sub-projects from a master project.

4 Use Edit > Delete Task

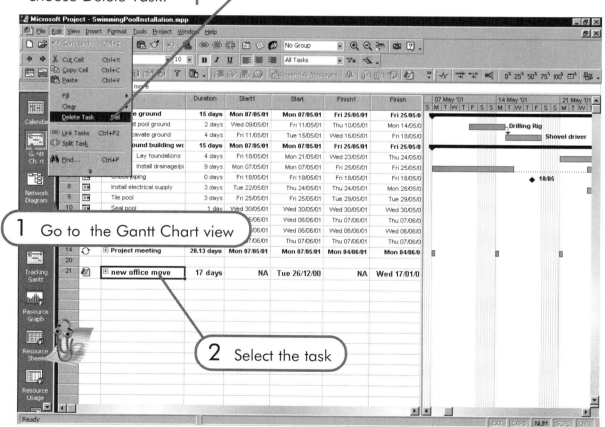

1 Go to the Gantt Chart view

2 Select the task

Linking tasks – opening multiple project files

The likelihood is that, if your organisation is working on more than one project, or if a complex project has been split into component sub-projects, there will be a requirement to create task dependencies between different projects. Put simply, this means that a task in one project will depend on a task from another project. This task could be a work task, in that a person with a specialist skill may be working on two projects, or a piece of machinery might be required to be shared between multiple projects to reduce hire or lease costs.

Linking tasks between projects is very similar to linking tasks within a single project. The main difference is that tasks linked from another project are shown in grey.

1 From the File menu, choose Open.

2 Select your first project file and click on Open.

3 Repeat steps 1 and 2 and open a further project file.

Tip

To check which project files are currently open, click on the Window menu and all open project files are listed.

Basic steps

1 Open the Window menu and choose Arrange All.

❑ Both open projects are now in view.

2 Select the task to link with another project.

3 Click the Task Information icon.

4 Open the Predecessors tab.

5 In the Task Name field, type the name of the project holding the task, followed by a back slash (\) and the task number in the holding project (note the task is shown as an External Task).

6 Press [Enter].

7 Click OK.

❑ Project 2000 inserts the linked task from the external project and shows it (in grey) in the task list and Gantt Chart view.

Linking tasks between project files

It's best to view multiple projects on screen before linking tasks. This then allows you to see a link between two tasks as you create it.

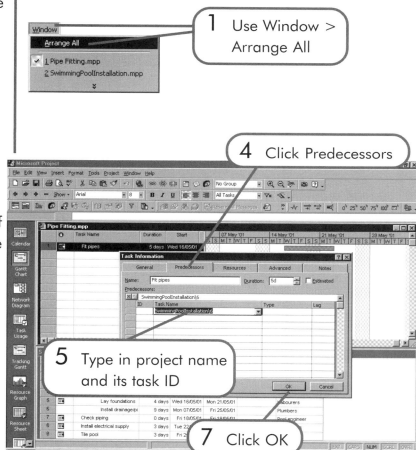

1 Use Window > Arrange All

4 Click Predecessors

5 Type in project name and its task ID

7 Click OK

Take note

All options for managing a task in a single project are available, even if tasks are linked between more than one project.

Summary

❑ A master project is a consolidation of individual sub-projects.

❑ Sub-projects are independent projects in their own right.

❑ Tasks can be linked between two projects.

❑ A resource pool allows you to share resources across multiple projects.

12 Sharing information

Copy Picture 126

Linking with Word 128

Saving projects as HTML 130

Inserting an image 131

Summary 132

Copy Picture

Sharing project information created in Project 2000 is a necessity. With the large number of application packages available that can carry out multiple functions, the flexibility to share information is now becoming vital. Project 2000 provides a number of ways to export project information, the very simplest being copying and pasting a displayed view.

Basic steps

1 Choose an appropriate view.

2 Click Copy Picture.

3 In the Render image area select *For screen*.

4 Click OK.

5 Switch to another application (e.g. WordPad).

6 From the Edit menu, choose Paste.

❑ The copied image is displayed.

Tip

You can also paste the image by using the [Ctrl]+[V] key strokes.

1 Choose a view

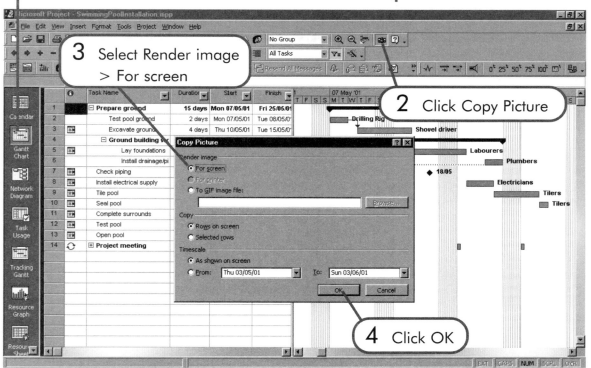

3 Select Render image > For screen

2 Click Copy Picture

4 Click OK

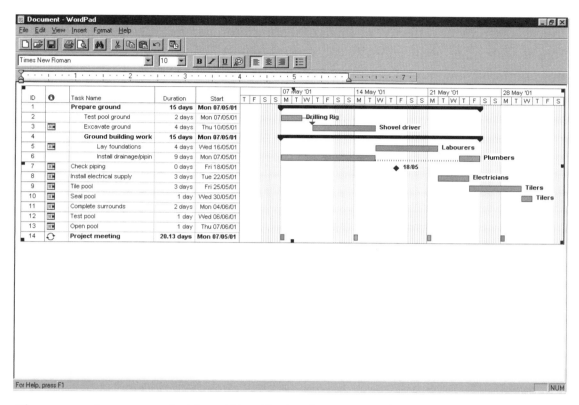

The screen image copied into WordPad, where it can be incorporated into a report. Images can be imported in the same way into other applications, such as PowerPoint presentations.

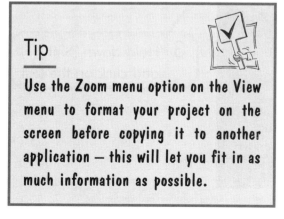

Tip

Use the Zoom menu option on the View menu to format your project on the screen before copying it to another application — this will let you fit in as much information as possible.

Take note

The copied data is treated as a single entity in the receiving application and cannot be easily edited.

Linking with Word

Project 2000 provides effective methods of sharing information from it with other applications in the Office suite. Linking project information into Microsoft's proprietary word processor, Word, is one of the simplest and most useful. Information can then be incorporated into fully formatted project reports and other documents.

Basic steps

❏ To copy fields

1 Select a sheet view.

2 Click on the heading of the first column.

3 Hold down [Shift] and click on the heading of the last column.

❏ To copy non-adjacent columns, hold [Ctrl] while selecting them.

4 Click the Copy icon.

5 Open or switch to Word and from its Edit menu, choose Paste.

Take note

You can also use the Copy Picture icon to copy a view into a Word document.

4 Click Copy

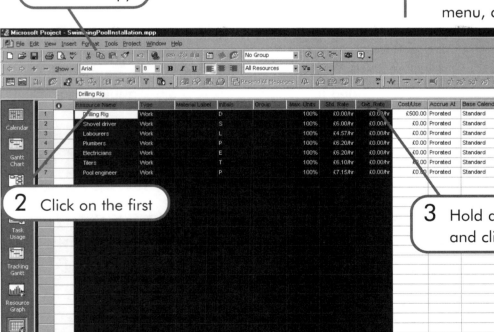

2 Click on the first

3 Hold down [Shift] and click on the last

Linking and embedding in Word

1 Select and copy the columns as shown opposite.

2 Open Word.

3 Place the insertion point at the point where you wish to insert project data.

4 Choose Paste Special from the Edit menu.

5 To embed the file select Paste.

Or

6 To link the file, select Paste link.

7 Click OK.

Linking allows you to add Project 2000 information into a Word document and have it dynamically updated. This means that any changes made to the original Project 2000 file will be reflected in the Word document containing the linked data. You can also choose to simply embed project information into a Word document where the embedded data will operate independently of the original Project 2000 file.

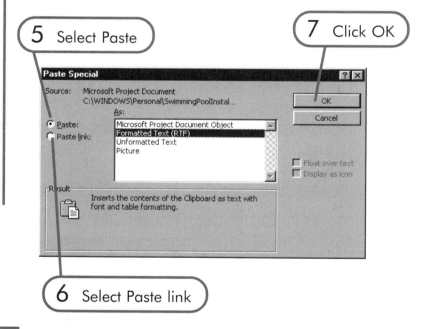

5 Select Paste

7 Click OK

6 Select Paste link

Take note

To copy Project 2000 data to other Office applications, follow the same procedures as described above.

Saving projects as HTML

With the need to share information ever more prevalent, the Web provides a great way to do this. Project 2000 allows you to save your project file as a Web page (in HTML format), ready for uploading. It does this through an export map. Experiment with other maps to determine the best one of your own needs. Each exports a different subset of your project's data.

Basic steps

1 From the File menu, choose Save As Web Page.

2 Choose a folder.

3 Name your HTML file.

4 Click Save.

5 From the Export Mapping dialog box select Export to HTML using standard template.

6 Click Save.

☐ Open your HTML file in your browser.

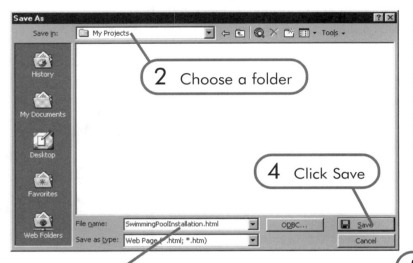

2 Choose a folder

4 Click Save

3 Give the file a name

5 Select Export to HTML...

6 Click Save

Take note

Once you've saved your project as HTML, use FTP software to upload the file to your Web site.

Basic steps

❑ Adding an image

1 Select the Gantt Chart view.

2 Copy an image into the Clipboard from your graphics package.

3 Click on the Gantt Chart bar area where you want the image.

4 From the Edit menu, choose Paste. The image is displayed.

Inserting an image

Project information and reports can often be enhanced by the inclusion of a suitable graphic image such as a company logo. Project 2000 allows you to place images grabbed from other applications and place them in graphic areas of the project.

Graphic areas include:

● Headers, footers and legends

● Gantt Chart bar area

● Task, resource and assignment notes areas.

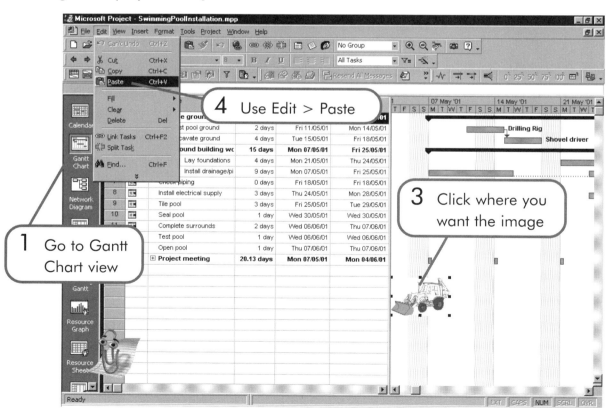

131

Summary

❑ Project 2000 information can be reported in a number of useful formats.

❑ Dynamic linking of Project 2000 information can be developed between it and other Office applications.

❑ Subsets of project data can be exported to HTML.

❑ Inserting an image in a project file can enhance its appearance.

Index

A

Accruals 112
Assignment views 16
Assignments 51
Assumptions 34
AutoFilter 103
AutoSave 13

B

Base calendar 49
Baselines 6, 72, 106

C

Calendar 9, 49
    multiple-base 50
Calendar view 17, 92
Closing Project 2000 13
Column
    add 80
    hide 81
Constraints 62
    adding to tasks 63
Copy Picture 126
Creating a file 2
Critical path 41
Critical task 41

D

Deleting tasks and sub-projects 121
Deliverables 34
Dependencies 58

E

Effort driven scheduling 53
Embedding in Word 129

F

Field names 82
Fields 80
Filename 5
Filters 101, 102

F

Finish to finish link 59
Fiscal year 20
Fixed Cost Accruals 112
Fixed rate, resource rate 70
Formatting
    Gantt Charts 85
    linked tasks 86
    text 84

G

Gantt Chart view 7, 18
GanttChart Wizard 31, 86

H

Headers and footers 75
Help 26
    on the Web 30
Hourly rate 66
HTML, saving as 130

I

Images 131
Interim plans 109

K

Keywords 4, 27

L

Lag times 60
Lead times 60
Links 59

M

Master project 116
    viewing 119
Material resources 44
Milestone 35
Multiple projects 116

N

Network diagram view 21, 93
Nodes 21

O

Objectives 34
Office Assistant 29
Opening Project 2000 2
Over-allocation 23, 54
Overtime rate 66

P

Passwords 6
Print Preview 12
Printing 12
Progress tracking 107
Project assignments 51
Project calendar 9
Project charts 90
Project costs, monitoring 113
Project scope 34
Project tasks, monitoring 110
Properties 4

R

Recurring tasks 36
Reports 74
Resource cost 69
Resource Graph view 95
Resource levelling 54
Resource lists 45
    sharing 46
Resource Name Form 96
Resource names 79
Resource pool 47
Resource rates 66
    fixed 70
Resource Sheet view 94
Resource Usage view 100
Resource views 16
Resources
    assign to calendar 52
    assigning multiple 53
    removing 53

S

Saving a project 5, 6
ScreenTips 28
Share Resources 46
Start to finish link 59
Start to start link 59
Sub-tasks 38
Summary tasks 37

T

Tables, modifying 83
Task Details form 98
Task ID 8
Task list 35
    outlining 38
Task names 78
Task usage view 22, 97
Task views 16
Tasks
    adding 8
    duration 10
    linking 58, 122
    notes 11
    sorting 87
    splitting 40
Timescales, changing 19
Tracking Gantt view 99

U

Update Tasks button 108

V

Views 16

W

Wage rate rises 71
Wizards 31
Word, linking with 128
Work resources 44
Working times 9
Write reservation 6